# I Need Your Hello

## STORIES OF HOPE & COMPASSION
## FROM THE REBUILD CENTER
## IN NEW ORLEANS

Compiled by Vicki Judice

Edited by Mary Rickard

Copyright @ 2022 by Vicki Judice

ISBN: 978-1-716-82614-6

Edited by Mary Rickard

Cover and text design by Anna Koeferl

Cover photograph by Bernie Saul

"Angel Fredricka" by Diana Harmon Jackson

"I Need Your Hello" title and story by Bruce Vara

## Photo Credits
Bernie Saul contributed many of the photographs included in the book. Other photographs were provided courtesy of the Clarion Herald, the Harry Tompson Center, Depaul USA, B.B. St. Roman and Lantern Light Ministry. All photos not specifically credited were contributed by the Harry Tompson Center, Lantern Light or Depaul USA.

## Proceeds
All proceeds from the sale of this book will go to benefit the St. Joseph Rebuild Center in New Orleans.

# Acknowledgements

After two years of compiling, writing, and editing, the time has come to share stories from the Rebuild Center with others. I greatly appreciate everyone who responded to my call to share one of their own accounts for this book. Four stories I wrote from my own personal experience. I compiled and edited the other narratives as they were told or given to me.

Thank you to the Rebuild Center directors who contributed and collected stories for the book: Jessica Lovell of Depaul USA, Emily Bussen Wain of the Harry Tompson Center, Kenitha Grooms-Williams of Lantern Light Ministry, and Fr. Thomas Stehlik of St. Joseph Parish. Many thanks to Bernie Saul who donated her professional time to take photographs for the book including the one used for the cover. Paisleigh Kelley of the Harry Tompson Center found photos from agency archives and was a cheerleader for the project.

Of particular significance is the contribution of stories from Bruce Vara, Hal Jefferson, Juston Winfield, Kevin Wilson, and Louis Herrera, who shared personal accounts of hardship, growth, and resilience. Their courage inspires me daily. Special recognition must be given to Bruce Vara whose story title "I Need Your Hello" was used with permission for the book's title. I owe a debt of gratitude to Bruce, as his story initially gave me the idea to compile and write other tales about the center.

Special thanks to volunteer Loretta Whyte and her friend Marilyn Wenzel who met with me in the early stages of the book's development to offer input on structure and content.

I am very grateful to my editor Mary Rickard. Her guidance, determination, care, and insistence on quality writing were invaluable.

Thank you to my son Joseph Koeferl who provided excellent suggestions for wording, formatting, and additional edits. Thank you to my daughter Anna Koeferl for designing the cover. I am grateful to Diana Harmon Jackson for creating the angel "Fredricka" featured on the cover and to my son Luke Koeferl, who created the linocut of St. Joseph's Church featured in the book's introduction.

Thank you to Fr. Louis Arceneaux for contributing information about St. Vincent de Paul from his article "Vincentians in New Orleans: A Mission to Serve" written in April 2017 and to Fr. Thomas Stehlik for contributing information about St. Vincent de Paul from the St. Joseph Parish website; to Sr. Vera Butler for contributing information about Nano Nagel in her article "Nano Nagel: Lady of the Lantern" written in July 2021; and to Vincent Bernard Liberto for permission to use information about Fr. Harry Tompson from his book <u>A Shepherd for New Orleans: Essays in honor of Rev. Harry W. Tompson, S.J.</u> written in 2002.

To all past and present supporters of the Rebuild Center – board members, guests, staff members, volunteers, prayer-givers, donors, funders, community partners – you rock! It is because of you that the Rebuild Center has become and continues to be such a meaningful and transformational place.

I am blessed to be part of such a life-giving community. So many close friends, family members and colleagues cheered me on to complete this project and I appreciate each and every one of you.

Lastly, I want to thank my loving husband John Koeferl, whose daily support helped me to believe in myself and to believe that I would indeed one day finish this book.

# CONTENTS

# Introduction

As so many already know, the Rebuild Center at St. Joseph's Church in New Orleans is a place where lives are transformed. The center – a collaboration between the Harry Tompson Center, Lantern Light Ministry, Depaul USA and St. Joseph's Church – has created a nurturing environment where people from various backgrounds, income levels and housing status meet, share resources, and get to know each other on a personal level. It is a place where amazing experiences have occurred over the years, resulting in stories not easily forgotten.

Miracles occur daily at the Rebuild Center. In the safety of a beautiful, shaded courtyard, people facing extraordinarily difficult challenges are welcomed and shown true care and concern. The center is a treasure, a "beloved community," filled with nourishment, love, and healing.

Throughout the seven years serving as director of the Harry Tompson Center, I was astounded time and time again by the guests' stories, which challenged my perceptions of poor and unhoused people. The experiences ultimately inspired and gifted me with the belief that we are more alike than we are different and upheld the vision that the world can become a better place when people from different backgrounds come together to share compassion for one another.

The Rebuild Center's mission is "to provide a safe environment, resources and opportunities for collaboration among Catholic and other faith-based organizations in the City of New Orleans for the service of those in need, together in one location."

The center provides an umbrella of daytime services to the hungry and unhoused, including nutrition (meals, groceries), hygiene and health (showers, shaving sinks, bathrooms, haircuts, medical care, psychiatric care), communication (phones, mail service, identification document assistance) and professional services (case management, linkages with income benefits, legal assistance, housing placement, long-term housing solutions).

Just as importantly, the Rebuild Center provides a dignified, daytime respite from the streets and harassment, so that those who are without homes or who are disadvantaged in some way may feel safe and respected.

## How did it all begin?

The Harry Tompson Center had been serving homeless people as a day shelter in a rented space next to the Jesuit church, Immaculate Conception, in downtown New Orleans since 1999. After Hurricane Katrina, 80 percent of the city's structures, including the Harry Tompson Center, flooded and could not reopen at that location, so representatives sought an alternate space. Coincidentally, Sr. Vera Butler and Lantern Light Ministry, which had been operating a Feed Jesus Program from a trailer behind St. Joseph's Church, planned to expand its own services. Likewise, the Vincentians of St. Joseph who were staffing the church wanted to broaden their ministry to the poor and unhoused by offering property for this purpose. It was destiny the three would unite their efforts to serve the unhoused and those in need.

On one pivotal afternoon in January 2006, representatives of the Harry Tompson Center, St. Joseph's Parish, Lantern Light Ministry, and UNITY of Greater New Orleans, the local homeless services collaborative, met to explore ways to fill the gap in services left by the Harry Tompson Center closing.

The meeting included Mary Baudouin, provincial assistant for social ministries for the Jesuits of the New Orleans Province; Fr. Ron Boudreaux, SJ, interim pastor of Immaculate Conception Parish; Fr. Perry Henry, CM, pastor of St. Joseph's Church; Sr. Vera Butler, PBVM, director of Lantern Light Ministries, and me, serving as deputy director of UNITY of GNO at the time.

The group committed to pursue the establishment of a new and improved center that would expand beyond the services previously offered by the Harry Tompson Center and Lantern Light Ministry. Fr. Boudreaux, an architect, suggested purchasing trailers for showers, bathrooms, and a multipurpose office that could be quickly installed on the back parking lot of St. Joseph's Church and connected by decking.

Mary Baudouin reached out to the University of Detroit Mercy's School of Urban Design and to local architect Wayne Troyer, who both agreed to help design the shelter. Mary and colleague Katy Quigley shepherded the fundraising capital campaign for the building project over the next 2 years. Former Harry Tompson Center director, Don Thompson, served as the primary construction manager for the project and helped to bring the plan into reality. One of the blessings of Hurricane Katrina was that groups from all across the country were willing to donate volunteers and funds for construction.

**St. Joseph's Rebuild Center is born!**

Following 21 months of intensive labor and a $1.1 million fundraising campaign, the Rebuild Center opened on September 11, 2007. During the first few years of operation, Catholic Charities Archdiocese of New Orleans also provided services at the center to the Hispanic community, which had grown after Hurricane Katrina.

Depaul USA joined the efforts in 2012, providing permanent supportive housing services for the chronically homeless population. For many years, the Tulane Canal Neighborhood Development Corporation also based its offices there.

Although each partnering organization specializes in particular services, together they are able to meet many of the basic and emergency needs of homeless and disadvantaged guests, as well as longer-term needs, such as housing and mental health counseling.

These services had been utilized by over 5,000 individuals annually, up until the COVID pandemic. The number of visitors has decreased due to city-mandated health constraints and a concerted effort led by UNITY of GNO and city/state representatives to house hundreds of people who had been sleeping on the streets.

## That place is for you

Sr. Enid Storey described an incident, highlighting the ultimate value of the Rebuild Center. When it was being constructed, a man walking by who appeared to be homeless asked, "Who is that place for?" She replied, "That place is for you." Suddenly, he began crying, saying, "Nobody ever built a place just for us."

Although set on a parking lot, the Rebuild Center is a beautiful space. The greenery of jasmine, palms, and bamboo amidst wooden decking provides visitors with a sense of openness, while still leaving space for privacy. The center embodies a calming spirit.

The architectural design and non-discriminatory attitude of staff and volunteers demonstrate respect for each person's dignity and worth. For those who have passed days without a shower, a meal, or even a conversation, the center is a welcoming oasis that offers respite, services, personal contact with those who sincerely care, and a real chance to improve their lives.

## The Founders

We stand on the shoulders of those who came before us. It is the work and vision of three significant Catholic leaders over the last several centuries which would ultimately lead to the creation of what we know now as "the Rebuild Center." It is important to take a moment to reflect on the significance of the Catholic leaders who can be considered the Rebuild Center's original founders: St. Vincent de Paul, Nano Nagel and Father Harry Tompson.
By recognizing their contributions and recalling their witness, we continue to be inspired to carry on the mission that they began so long ago.

## St. Vincent de Paul – Father of the Poor

Vincentians.org

The earliest of the founders was St. Vincent de Paul, who founded the Vincentian order of Catholic priests in France in the 1600s. He is sometimes referred to as the "Apostle of Charity" and the "Father of the Poor." From Fr. Louis Arceneaux's article "Vincentians in New Orleans: A Mission to Serve," we learn about St. Vincent de Paul and the Vincentians' impact in our region.

The Vincentians were extremely influential in the European settling of Southern Louisiana in the 1800s. They established many parishes including St. Stephen's Parish in New Orleans in 1849. Later in 1858, the Vincentians began to serve in St. Joseph's Parish. The existing church structure of St. Joseph Church was dedicated in 1892.

Graphic by Luke Koeferl

Over time, the Vincentians have been involved in numerous ministries in New Orleans. They have served as hospital chaplains at Charity Hospital, Hotel Dieu, Touro, and many other health care facilities. Their presence has sparked numerous ministries for the poor, including the parish-led St. Vincent de Paul Societies and ultimately, the Rebuild Center.

The Vincentian Family in New Orleans is far-reaching and includes many members, all dedicated to serving the poor in the local Catholic Archdiocese and supporting others in that service: Daughters of Charity, Sisters of Charity, Ladies of Charity, Society of St. Vincent de Paul, and Depaul USA.

# Nano Nagle– Lady of the Lantern

Our second founder established the Presentation Sisters of the Blessed Virgin Mary to educate and care for the poor in 18th century Ireland.

In her article "Nano Nagel – Lady of the Lantern," Sr. Vera Butler details how that ministry would result in the establishment of Lantern Light Ministry in New Orleans 250 years later.

Presentationsisters.org

Nano Nagle's dream was to form a dedicated group of women to educate those who were poor and destitute and perform "lantern works." On Christmas Eve 1775, Nano's own congregation of sisters was established - the Sisters of Charitable Instruction of the Sacred Heart of Jesus. When the Order was approved by Rome in 1805, the name of the congregation was changed to "Presentation Sisters of the Blessed Virgin Mary."

Nano became well known as the "Lady of the Lantern" and her sisters were called "Nano's Walking Nuns" because, like Nano, they walked the streets of Cork, bringing assistance and comfort to those who were most in need. Nano Nagle died April 26, 1784. Her last words to the small group of sisters at her bedside were, "Love one another as you have hitherto done. Spend yourselves for the poor."

This is the spirit that energized and inspired the Presentation Sisters for centuries as they have continued to serve the destitute. It was this spirit that attracted Sr. Vera Butler to respond to the request from St. Joseph's Church and the Vincentians in 1998 to coordinate their outreach programs and which ultimately led to the creation of Lantern Light Ministry in 2005.

## Father Harry Tompson, S.J.

Fr. Harry William Tompson was born in New Orleans in 1936. From Vincent Liberto's book <u>A Shepherd for New Orleans: Essays in honor of Rev. Harry W. Tompson, S.J.</u>, we learn that Fr. Tompson helped to create many social ministries which still exist today in New Orleans.

Photo courtesy of the Clarion Herald

Growing up in the Algiers neighborhood, Harry attended Holy Name of Mary Elementary School and was taught by the Marianites of Holy Cross. After attending Jesuit High School, he entered the Jesuit Order at St. Charles College in Grand Coteau, Louisiana in 1954 and was ordained a priest by Archbishop Philip M. Hannan at Holy Name of Jesus Church in New Orleans in 1967.

For the next 33 years, he served in various capacities including teacher at Jesuit College Preparatory in Dallas, dean of students at Strake Jesuit College Preparatory in Houston, teacher, president and principal of Jesuit High School in New Orleans, director of Manresa Retreat House in Convent and pastor of Immaculate Conception Parish in downtown New Orleans.

During the time from 1994 to his death in 2001, Fr. Tompson worked to set up structures that would bring favorable economic conditions to neighborhoods most in need. His efforts culminated in the founding of Good Shepherd School, Café Reconcile, and the Harry Tompson Center, all of which still exist today.

Fr. Tompson's life has impacted thousands over the years. Through his embodiment of Jesuit values, he empowered people to strengthen their love for others and be of better service to those in need. Today, 21 years after his death, that same spirit of hospitality and care for the poor lives on in the people he touched and in all the ministries he helped establish.

## The Stories

There are so many remarkable personal, life-affirming experiences which have occurred at the Rebuild Center since its inception in 2007. This book selects a mere 45, some spanning several months, but most happening in just a few minutes.

Most of the tales offered in this book are told from the perspective of a staff member or volunteer whose encounter with a Rebuild Center guest sparked some reflection or insight. Visitors receiving services at the center are called "guests" instead of "clients" to emphasize their dignity and inherent worth.

Five narratives have been written by formerly homeless persons who were guests at the center. Some were written by people with advanced education degrees, while others were told by people with little formal schooling.

What all the tales have in common is that they meant something very important to the teller and created a significant change in their lives. The book's 45 stories witness to the power of a place where people can come together and experience the love of God no matter their history or situation. They tell of a sacred place where fear of the stranger is overcome and the "other" becomes "one another", and the dignity and sanctity of each human life is co-respected and celebrated.

While all the events in this book are true, most of the names of the guests have been changed to protect their identities.

These stories are for you. I hope that they may be of positive benefit to you, no matter what your life circumstances may be at this particular time. I hope they may offer a bit of tenderness, compassion, and optimism for the future of our world.

# CHAPTER ONE: GREETINGS

Photo by Bernie Saul

*"You see that Mary statue right there? She's broken. And I'm broken.*

*And when I need to, I sit with her, and that brings me comfort.*

*It gives me strength."*

- *Guest*

Photos courtesy of The Clarion Herald

Photos courtesy of Bernie Saul

# There Is a Harmony
By Jessica Lovell

My workday starts when I round the corner of the parking lot and head toward the front entrance of the Rebuild Center. There, waiting for the doors to open at 8 a.m., is a line of men and women. A series of "Good Mornings" and other "Hellos" are heard as I make my way to the entrance. The crowd thickens as I approach the front doors and, inevitably, one of our guests steps in to clear a path and push me in my wheelchair into the center and all the way up the ramp, then heads back out front to wait until 8 a.m. with the rest of the guests.

Since I started at the center, I have been so humbled by the generosity of people who have so little yet graciously give so much. Each day, I witness acts of selflessness and compassion among guests, staff, and volunteers alike. It is not uncommon for a perfect stranger to advocate on behalf of their neighbor, simply based on an understanding of the difficulties of homelessness and the complications that it causes. I feel like I have learned from so many, how to be a better person and have a greater appreciation for humanity.

Here is an example I want to share, not uncommon at the center. During one of the first very cold days in 2016, we were giving out winter hats just after lunch. After the last hat was handed out, a guy walked up and asked for one, but was sadly told there were no more. Another homeless gentleman took the hat he was just given off of his head and gave it to the stranger standing in front of him, knowing the temperature would fall to the 30s at night. Sincere gratitude and thanks were returned in favor, and I went off to try and scrounge up another hat, finding a scarf instead.

I like to think of the center as imperfectly beautiful, unique, and balanced. There is a harmony that exists in the space that is the Rebuild Center. An abundance of acceptance and love (though often tough love) flows there and helps create an atmosphere that allows people to feel safe. The high regard and appreciation that guests feel for the Rebuild Center, staff, and volunteers gives our jobs immense purpose and meaning.

The flip side of this is a harsh reality. Many days at the center can be challenging, both emotionally and mentally. There is never a shortage of sad stories and sometimes seemingly unsolvable problems. Yet even on these days, Charlie shows up with a new 'Everybody Loves Charlie' drawing to hang in your office. You know Wayne is there because you can hear his voice from inside, and he gifts you with laughter and love. Terry walks all the way to the center on your birthday just to wish you a happy birthday. And there is always someone who says thank you for saying hello, smiling, being kind, listening, being helpful, or just understanding during these difficult days.

On this note, I cannot leave out the incredibly loving, caring, and simply amazing people that I work with. They truly build my spirits (and others') and make me a better person. There exists a small but mighty family at the Rebuild Center, and I am both grateful and proud to be a part of it!

# I Need Your Hello
By Bruce Vara

It must have been after lunch because I don't remember a whole lot of people around and I was sitting on the long bench across from the meeting room and kitchen area. I had the whole place to myself - practically unheard of, knowing how crowded Rebuild can be. I must have had a doctor's appointment or a meeting with my caseworker, Andrew, because I don't often hang out after lunch either. To pass the time, I was reading a book, just enjoying the quiet and solitude, but that didn't last long as I found myself a front-row spectator to one of the most unselfish Christian acts I've ever witnessed. I can say without a doubt, it literally changed my life.

It involved one of my fellow guests at the Rebuild Center whom I don't know by name or history. I just have seen him around town and here to know him by sight. I had never heard him speak. He seemed to me quiet and gentle - definitely not a troublemaker. But lo and behold a very dedicated case worker saw him and let's just say, it was on! "You've been ducking me for two days and that's not working! I need your hello! This is important - **I need your hello**," the case worker nearly shouted at him.

Now to you, this outburst might seem harsh, unjustified or maybe, unprofessional. But in no way at all was it given with even a touch of rancor, anger, or meanness. In no way, was this meant to humiliate the guest, to embarrass him or make him feel less worthy. But in reality, her strong words were meant to uplift him by demonstrating true concern.

I saw empathy defined: love, warmth, understanding, compassion, heartfelt acknowledgement of another's worth - regardless of race, creed, or gender. The guest stood motionless except with his head bobbing up and down. Although not exactly a verbal "hello," his nodding head was his way of saying he would accept the help offered him. They were a team, without one being a giver or one being a taker, but in joint effort to accomplish whatever was necessary to improve his situation. "I'm here and I need your hello!" Plain and simple.

Inspired, I wrote a children's book titled, "I Need Your Hello!" yet unpublished, but there is always hope, regardless of how many rejections.

I saw unselfish Christianity at work that day, which I will never forget nor will I ever be able to repay this case worker for what she taught me that day – that sometimes what is required is to let others know you care about them with a loud, determined and persistent voice.

Thank you to her, thank you to the Rebuild Center and Thank God! Amen. Peace.

# Blessings in Disguise
By Sr. Suzanne Anglim

After over a year of forced hiatus due to COVID-19, I was eager to return to the Rebuild Center for my morning volunteer service. Volunteering there consists of my simply visiting with the guests who choose to share their stories with me. This conversation might occur anywhere – on a curb outside or on a bench inside the center.

One recent fine spring day, I returned to volunteer. Looking around the center, I couldn't help but notice the changes that had occurred during the pandemic. Our once bustling courtyard, alive with the chatter of nearly 200 guests, looked sparse. Gone were the old ways of free-flowing movement and roaming between resource stations. Instead, arrows pointed to entries and exits, orange cones marked appropriate places to sit, and the sunrise shower service operated with more regiment than ever. It was a different place but had found its rhythm. As I took in the sights, something caught my eye.

"Mercy," I thought, "She's broken." The statue of the Virgin Mary that sat nestled near the front entrance of the courtyard was cracked in a few places and the garden was overgrown with weeds. I couldn't help but feel a little distraught over this. What had happened to this statue to cause its disrepair? When you care about others you want to have a good, caring environment for them. Did this statue need to be fixed or replaced? My thoughts buzzed. I decided to pray on the issue and let it rest until God could show me the answer.

During my volunteer shift the next week, I made my normal rounds at the center, greeting each guest with a "good morning." Some ignored me, others simply nodded without looking up. I listened and looked for that graced moment when a guest might return my salutation. When I made eye contact, I asked if I could sit down with them. Then the magic began. I started by listening to whatever they wanted to talk about and then, I asked questions about what helped get them through their days.

This morning, when a guest returned my greeting, I asked if I could sit down with her. We sat on the bench directly in front of the statue of the Virgin Mary. I asked my usual questions: "What keeps you going? What gives you hope each day?" The woman replied, "You see that Mary statue right there? She's broken. And I'm broken. And when I need to, I sit with her, and that brings me comfort. It gives me strength."

I sat in amazement. Was this the answer from God that I'd been waiting for? I considered the idea that perhaps I'd been thinking about the statue all wrong – perhaps others saw Mary's brokenness as a blessing. I was moved and humbled, but not altogether convinced that the statue shouldn't be repaired.

The next Monday when I returned for my volunteer shift, I again approached guests in the courtyard. Another "good morning" was returned, allowing me to sit and chat with a regular attendee, an older gentleman.

Again, I asked my usual questions. "What keeps you going? What gives you hope each day?" Uncannily, he responded, "When I need help, I come visit with Mary." He gestured toward the statue on the other side of the courtyard.

"Her brokenness reminds me that even the most perfect people are not perfect. God didn't make us perfect, and it helps me get by."

Here I was, trying to fix something when all I needed to do was listen. Our guests teach me things all the time. The broken Mary statue wasn't an eyesore or a burden to them. She is a symbol of their struggle, my struggle and the human struggle - it is what connects all of us to a sense of hope.

Sometimes it's not what we can do for someone else; it's being available to be with them where they are.

# Incident of the Towels
By Mike O'Connell

On a beautiful afternoon in late August 2018, I was washing towels for our shower service when a guest, Mr. James, knocked on the laundry room door. When I opened it, a loud Mr. James yelled at me, "Hey, man, you stole my towels!" "I stole your towels?" I asked. "Yeah man, those were my towels on the ground there and I use them to sleep on. I sleep on them here and at night. You don't see anyone else in here sleeping on towels, do you?"

I apologized, saying that I thought they were towels to be laundered for the showers. Even when I picked them up, I was unsure, but they looked like the shower towels. Mr. James replied, "No, man, those were *my* towels. And not only that, I collect towels at the hotels and then I donate extra towels here." Although I was uncertain of the truth of Mr. James' statements (and simultaneously worried that I had stolen his towels), I sincerely apologized and said that I would return the towels to him as soon as they were dry. Mr. James accepted my apology and, shortly thereafter, the clean towels.

At the time, I was the new Jesuit Volunteer at the Harry Tompson Center. I was responsible for coordinating the showers in the morning, including cleaning the showers and towels with the help of the world-class volunteers. I had only served two weeks of my year commitment and was just beginning to learn the guests' names and stories. Yet, I was already becoming familiar with Mr. James through his vibrant personality.

Mr. James is a very vocal male in his 50s. At the time of the towel incident, he slept on the streets and, as he stated, on top of his towels. Mr. James is a big Saints fan and a gig economy worker. For example, Mr. James sells beads on Bourbon Street and resells Jazz Fest tickets that he's collected by walking down Bourbon Street at 7 a.m. in the morning.

Whenever Mr. James entered the Rebuild Center, he made his presence known by yelling "Hello!" to each staff member as he came across them. For example, Emily, assistant director at the time, had just returned from maternity leave and Mr. James greeted her loudly, "Ms. Emily, how's that little bumblebee?!" This greeting always made everyone around laugh or smile.

On occasion, Mr. James brought his radio and played music for everyone. As I was responsible for the shower list, he'd always yell, "Hey Mike! Put me on stand-by!" I quickly learned this meant, depending on his day, Mr. James may or may not shower when I got to his name. Although Mr. James never complained to me about not getting a shower due to length of the wait list or his being asleep when called, he was certainly both upset and understanding when I stole and cleaned his towels on that sunny August day.

A few weeks later, late September, I walked into work on a Monday morning and found a large black garbage bag at the top of the steps. It was filled with an assortment of different sized white towels and sheets! While I was a bit surprised, I was confident that Mr. James had gotten them from the hotels. I was filled with joy! Mr. James had spoken the truth and we now had additional towels for our guests. When I saw Mr. James a few days later, I thanked him and, instead of saying "I told you so," he humbly responded that he would try to get more towels soon.

After the towel incident, my relationship with Mr. James improved and I would, secretly, assist him a bit more than other guests.

For example,

- Mr. James would ask me for the "hook up" and I would secretly prepare a bag with a T-shirt, underwear, socks, and shorts or sweatpants to give him before his shower.
- Mr. James would ask for beads (presumably to resell on Bourbon Street) and I would take them from the art supply closet.
- In early February 2019, I obliged when Mr. James brought a suit and shirt and asked me to wash them so he could wear them on his birthday.

Like many Rebuild Center guests, Mr. James did not have much income and met many of his basic needs there, such as showering, washing, and getting meals. Also, like many of the guests, Mr. James donated items he did not need personally, such as towels, to benefit others and the community. Although I originally (internally) questioned his honesty and generosity, the towel incident and subsequent donation proved Mr. James to be true to his word.

In February 2020, I returned to New Orleans and the Rebuild Center for the first time in six months. I learned Mr. James was happily housed with his new turtle through the help of the Harry Tompson Center's case management services. Further, I received an even bigger surprise: Mr. James marked down the day of my visit and greeted me in his loud, loving voice, "Hello, Mike!"

# Antonio Banderas
By Beth Monahan

One of the guests Lantern Light kitchen staff is always delighted to see is Victor, a.k.a. Antonio Banderas, Queen Elizabeth II, Sheik Abdul, and a host of other celebrities who occasionally drop in. As soon as Victor makes his appearance, the word goes out and volunteers flock to visit with him. He usually has a corny, sometimes incomprehensible joke to share, generating laughter because of Victor's glee and infectious giggle telling it.

Victor's dining requests vary with the character he happens to be on any given day. Antonio Banderas wants a sausage, egg and cheese sandwich on a croissant. Queen Elizabeth always wants a blueberry muffin and hot chocolate. Needless to say, he happily accepts whatever is given.

One of Victor's favorite foods is a banana because of its many uses. As a phone, he can call the Health Department to report an infraction. As a service weapon, he can arrest the lawless kitchen volunteer, although when he makes arrests, he always reads the accused their Miranda rights. He brandishes his banana weapon only to make arrests, never to commit a crime, and delights in devouring it afterwards so that all evidence is gone.

One day when winter was approaching, Victor made the comment that it was time to get arrested for public intoxication so he could go to jail until the weather got warmer. When the staff expressed skepticism that anyone in New Orleans would get arrested for public intoxication, he agreed and claimed that he intended to go to Atlanta and get arrested there. He then went on to explain what to do to get the judge to increase the sentence from 30 to 90 days so that the incarceration would last until spring. Of course, Victor was giggling the whole time he was telling his improbable story.

Since the onset of the pandemic, Victor has only come to the center a few times for very brief visits. When he last visited, he left an order for a tenderloin with béarnaise sauce, roasted potatoes, and grilled asparagus. If only that were possible!

Here is a man who apparently has no material possessions, no roof over his head, often doesn't know where his next meal will come from, yet still has a sense of humor and appears to be enjoying life.

God bless you, Victor. Hurry back to the center soon as we could all use a good laugh.

# Honey, I'm Home!
## By Bernadine Dupre

Once I heard that greeting, I knew that William had arrived at the center. William was one of the most gregarious people I have ever met - loud, brash, friendly, always in a good mood and always with a good story to tell you.

As a shower assistant, my job was to keep track of the shower list and call guests when it was their time to shower, give them soap and shampoo, assign them a stall and then clean it after each use. When I called William's name, he would inevitably call back in response, "Come on down!" or "The price is right!" or some other adage that would get a laugh out of me, no matter my mood that day. He was determined to make me laugh and bring some joy into my day. It always worked.

He was very fatherly, too, and made sure I was taking care of myself while volunteering at the center. "Where are your gloves? You can't clean those stalls without gloves!"

It turns out that I knew some members of his family as I had lived around the area where he grew up. Our lives were less separated than previously thought. He was about my same age– in my 60's – and I will never forget William's beautiful eyes.

William also helped with the monthly haircut services. He would sweep up the room after each haircut and make sure people weren't jumping the line, telling them when to come in and sit down. He took pride in the center and fussed whenever somebody threw trash on the ground.

William appreciated being able to take a shower every weekday at the Rebuild Center and didn't take it for granted. Like many others, getting a shower along with shower supplies, clean underwear, and a pair of socks were big luxuries and most appreciated for those who had jobs, were applying for jobs or needed to show up for a court date. Think about how you feel when you don't have a shower. It is a real game-changer.

We didn't know too much about why William had become homeless or where he was sleeping at night. But I was so happy to learn that when the Harry Tompson Center paid an old $101 water bill for him, he was able to move into senior housing.

While volunteering at the Rebuild Center to care for others, I didn't expect to feel cared for and shown compassion by one of the guests! The fact that William was looking after me and concerned about my safety took me by surprise, but made me realize that he, like many of our guests at the Rebuild Center, was just a regular human being who has feelings for others, too, and could be loving and kind. He was more than just a homeless person who needed help.

# The Pandemic
### By Kenitha Grooms-Williams

The pandemic has presented several challenges for many of our guests, including individuals enrolled in Lantern Light's Food Bank program.

Ms. Jackson started coming to our grocery distribution about five years ago, along with several other seniors who reside in an apartment complex near the center. As New Orleans faced its first case of COVID-19 during the second week of March 2020, Lantern Light raced to ensure that all our clients received groceries for the month. We informed Ms. Jackson and others that it was unclear how our organization would continue this service, but we would contact each client by phone once we established a plan.

As the next week brought more COVID cases and an eventual shutdown of the city, I began to consider ways we could continue to provide food and toiletry items to the families who relied on this service monthly. Recognizing the need for our clients to maintain social distancing, our agency decided that we would attempt to deliver items to three complexes, which were less than two miles away from our ministry. Our first steps would include making calls to the property manager of each apartment building to ensure their approval of our delivery, and then calls to each client notifying them of our plans to continue the food pantry operation. Keeping in mind the urgency of maintaining this service, we decided our first calls would be made to clients who were seniors.

When I contacted Ms. Jackson by phone, the excitement and relief in her voice was the first indication that delivering groceries would become more than just a temporary solution for a few months. Ms. Jackson shared that she was so grateful because she did not know how she was going to come to the center during the pandemic without risking her health. She further explained that she depends on the groceries and toiletry items that we have provided her for the past several years because she lives on fixed income and receives little assistance from the state's food stamp program.

While many of us assumed that the pandemic would end a few months after March, we ultimately realized that our lives would forever be changed. As time has gone by and high demand for food remains, Lantern Light continues to deliver groceries to Ms. Jackson and many other families in those three apartment complexes. Each month, when I drive to Ms. Jackson's complex, I am always greeted with a smile and heartfelt thanks, not just from her, but from other seniors in our food bank program.

Ms. Jackson never forgets to say thank you before she picks up her bags and always shares how much she appreciates our agency delivering these much-needed items to her.

# Salutations!
## By Paisleigh Kelley

Every day I see him at the center, Miles greets me with a warm "Salutations!" I ask how he slept and how he's doing. "Every day above ground is a good day," he replies.

We exchange pleasantries as he brushes his teeth and packs up his assortment of necessities – a sleeping pad, blanket, plastic bags of extra clothing, and more. He has a system, securing everything in just the right way so that his towering backpack can stay balanced as he goes about the day. He calls it his mobile home.

It is Miles' way with words and his relentless positivity that piques my interest. I want to understand how someone with so little can hold such a consistently optimistic worldview. Before he leaves, I ask if I can interview him. "If it helps people, then sure. We should do it," he replies.

On a frigid January morning, I meet Miles at the center with coffee and a blueberry muffin. We settle in against the wind and he begins to tell me about himself. He's in his early 30's and one of seven siblings. Although he didn't live with his mother, he reveres her strength and credits her as the source of his determination, independence, and positivity. His father and older brother were military men – a career he considered for some time, along with law and medicine.

In 2016, Miles had a 9-to-5 sales job in the Midwest. He had an apartment. A car. *A normal life*. But he had what he calls a "Tower" moment. In Tarot, the Tower card represents unforeseen change, often defined by a sense of danger, destruction, and liberation. Miles' Tower moment arrived when he was approached by several officers while walking to pay his rent. A murder had occurred in the area and police were on the lookout for a Black man. "That's all it takes for people like us," Miles says. Soon he was on the ground, several officers restraining him.

Police cuffed him and stripped his pockets, but Miles found it odd that they failed to remove his firearm, which was licensed, registered, and remained strapped in his holster. Officers stood to the side, whispering, Miles worried they might kill him. He saw blood on the ground and knew it was his but could not tell where it was coming from. "Dude, I have a firearm. Take it!" he demanded. Only then did the officers confiscate the gun. In the end, Miles was booked on charges of carrying a concealed weapon.

"Putting people behind bars is inhumane," Miles says, peeling back the paper skin of his muffin. "I spent nearly six weeks in jail and never committed a single crime." We don't talk much about his time in jail, but I can tell that it stays with him. Miles' father hired a lawyer, but even with legal representation, the courts pushed a plea deal. Miles stood his ground, knowing he had done nothing wrong.

In the end, Miles was able to prove that the arresting officer falsified his police report by showing the judge his purchase receipt for his holster. He was free but putting his life back together after missing nearly two months of work set him back.

Miles soon found himself evicted and moved in with his sister and father. Miles talks candidly about his experiences with homelessness. "What people don't realize is that everything we ingest becomes part of us. That's not just food, it's all things spiritual, social, economic. You gotta pay attention to what you give attention to. The way I live my life is that I consume, digest, and release. It's not a diet, it's a *live-it*. And that is with everything. I try to allow the nutrients to nourish me and the rest to pass me by." This is how Miles talks about most things, with little attachment to material items, money, or status and a high priority on lessons, memories, personal philosophy, and growth.

Miles and his sister had intended to move in together, but circumstances kept them apart. Instead, he travelled, sleeping on various friends' couches. It was a time of self-discovery and reflection. Eventually, his sister made good on their promise to live together, allowing Miles to move in with her and her boyfriend who had settled in New Orleans. Miles found work and ways to contribute to the household. Things held steady for some time, but eventually the landlord found out that there was an extra tenant, and he was kicked out. This marked his introduction to living on the streets.

Miles didn't have a lot of personal belongings, but he packed two bags of necessities and searched for a place to go. He ended up sleeping behind the dumpster at his job in Metairie. The first few nights were rough. I asked what it was like for him to adjust to sleeping outside.

"Survival instincts kick in. You learn that food, water, clothing and shelter are vital, and you figure it out. What is more important than dealing with the elements is taking care of your mind. The truth is that for anyone to grasp what it's like, you either have to go through it yourself or know someone who has."

Miles rarely asks for money, but at the gas station where he sits in the morning to charge his phone before work, strangers give him cash. Many tell him that they've been where he is. They tell him it will get better.

Miles made a habit of walking to and from his job, which he was able to keep until the pandemic hit. In the early aftermath of COVID-19, like so many others, he found himself unemployed and unable to find work. He began walking from Metairie to the nearest bus stop and downtown to navigate resources available to people who are unhoused. Now, he sleeps at various spots in the city. He says that he would stay at an overnight shelter if the weather got really bad but prefers to keep to himself.

For a few months after COVID-19 hit, Miles spent his days desperately filling out applications, trying to get hired, but at some point, that became fatiguing. Libraries and community centers that used to supply access to computers remain limited, if accessible at all, and Miles does not have much data he can use on his phone each month. Sometimes, he visits local coffee shops and checks in on applications. He keeps his clothing in decent shape and tries his best to blend in. Often, his mobile home (backpack) gives him away and authorities ask him to leave.

These days, Miles wakes up before sunrise. He meditates and hydrates before packing his bags and making his way to the center for his daily shower. He grabs a snack from the meal line and starts walking, looking for spaces where he might be allowed to stay and listen to music or watch inspirational videos on YouTube. He believes that the experience of homelessness is testing him, strengthening him, and preparing him for the next step. He has several job interviews lined up and is hopeful that one will work out.

Throughout the weekend following our interview, I find myself thinking about Miles and wondering what wisdom he would offer up as they relate to my personal challenges, which I can't help but see as miniscule in relation to his. I think about how Miles is only a year or so older than I am, and how scared I would be in his shoes. I admire him more for this – for his ability to stay present, resilient, positive, and patient, and for his willingness to share his story with others.

I make it part of my practice to envision him where Miles wants to be – traveling – and keep him in my heart as I move about the world. I make it my goal to promote the take-away Miles wants from our readers: we could all have a little more empathy.

A simple salutation could make all the difference.

# CHAPTER TWO: SAME LIKE ME

*"We are the same.*
*You could be one hospital bill away from homelessness."*

*-Juston Winfield*

Photo by Bernie Saul

Photos courtesy of Bernie Saul

Photos courtesy of Bernie Saul

# Maintaining Appearances

By Kevin Wilson

Eileen had been receiving laundry and shower services from us for several months when I noticed that she always kept herself very neat and well dressed. I wondered how she managed to do that given she had been sleeping outside awhile now. It brought back memories about my own life when I had to figure out how to maintain my appearance while sleeping outside.

After talking with her over the next few months, I found out a lot more about Eileen and what had caused her homelessness. I learned that this 55-year-old woman had been a victim of domestic violence that caused her homelessness. I learned that she feared for her life on the streets and so constantly moved her sleeping location from Duncan Plaza to City Park to the downtown library – to ensure a sense of safety, both from her abuser and strangers while living on the street.

I still wondered, how did she manage to survive these dark days yet still remain so positive and well-dressed?

I decided to make a point to ask her about this. She said that she was determined to hold onto this last bit of normalcy in her life – her cleanliness and appearance – to get her through these tough, dark days. The shower services that we offer at the Harry Tompson Center's satellite office at the Community Resource and Referral Center had helped her maintain dignity. Thanks to the generosity of donors, we could offer her a variety of clothing which aided her in restoring some normalcy.

In getting to know her, I was inspired by Eileen's strong resilience and motivation to overcome any obstacles that got in her way. She always believed that the best was yet to come and clung to that hope.

I'm happy to report that she did finally end her bout of homelessness and recently moved into permanent housing where she is doing well. I even heard her recently on the radio, speaking to a group about her ordeal of living on New Orleans' streets.

I realized that the common denominator between Eileen and me was our strong motivation to maintain our dignity and appearance no matter what we were going through. You see I, too, had been homeless and slept outside by the World Trade Center for almost two years before I sought and received the help I needed to find housing. And during those two long, tough years, I hung onto the hope that things would indeed get better one day. Meanwhile, I would avail myself of clothing and hygiene services to maintain my self-esteem and help for job interviews.

During that time, many people didn't believe that I was experiencing homelessness because of the way I dressed. I have not forgotten those days.

Now, I see people on the street who say "Hey Kevin, remember when we used to sit on the benches at the Oz during those long, hot summer months? You're one of the success stories now."

# It Can Happen to Anyone
By Liam Fitzgerald

A couple of months ago, someone I knew stumbled into the Rebuild Center. I graduated from Jesuit High School with his brother. Coming from a privileged background, this was the last person I thought I would see utilizing the services we provide to those without homes. Seeing him was a strong reminder that homelessness can happen to anyone.

I recognized him the moment I saw him across the courtyard, and the look he gave me said he recognized me, too. Instead of stopping to talk to him, I gave him a small smile and walked right past him, just as I would have had I seen him flying a sign on the street.

In my seven years around the center, I had never encountered a familiar face and it threw me for a loop. I never thought that one of those in need would include someone who had attended my same high school, a prestigious Catholic institution.

Students from those high schools come to volunteer every summer and it was shocking to see him there as a guest, instead. I wouldn't expect to see anyone like me out of options - outside of a support network.

I worked up the nerve to go talk to him a few minutes later and the first things I noticed were that he was without shoes and needed a shower, too. I asked him what he was doing at the center, and he told me that he had come to attend our weekly Share & Support meeting, a space for people struggling with life on the streets, to drink coffee together and talk.

He asked me what I was doing at the center, and I said I worked here. He was intrigued and asked me if I had ever come out to be with "the people." I responded that I stayed inside the center to work, indicating that I was not there to socialize. He seemed a little disappointed, almost like I was saying that he belonged out there and I belonged in here, which was not my intent, but I didn't know how else to respond.

That was the reality of our situations - he was spending his days and nights on the streets, and although I spend my days at the Rebuild Center, I get to go home to a family and a bed.

We often say, "homelessness could happen to anyone," and, as much as I can see that in other people's lives and stories, I have a hard time believing it could happen to me. This classmate of mine has a support network like mine, connections like mine, and a background like mine. If *he* ended up on the streets, this really could happen to anyone, even a Jesuit boy.

# Like Me, Like You
By Maggie and Sterling Millet

There have been many opportunities in our lives to give back through our church, the Girl Scouts, and as a teacher in a K-12 school, which had encouraged community service. As Christians, the Bible challenges us to reach out to those in need and to the ones living on the margins. Thus began our experience with the homeless.

As retirees, my husband Sterling and I were encouraged by our pastor, Fr. Tom Stehlik, to volunteer at the Rebuild Center. Lantern Light had just received a donation of laptop computers and the plan was to provide blocks of time for guests to use the computer room to learn the keyboard, do research and surf the internet, spending close to two hours in a quiet, calm, non-threatening atmosphere.

Each Monday, we arrived to set up the room, made a general announcement to guests that computers were available, and then began our day. Some participants were weekly regulars, yet others dropped in for just one day and didn't stay long. Others came just to charge their phones or get warm, but several guests stood out and remain in our memories.

Like Alfred. A regular with a smile and happy disposition, he was always looking for Sterling because they had an ongoing battle of the Steelers vs. the Saints. "When are you going to see the light and support the Steelers?" Alfred would tease. Each week, we helped him find the sports highlights. He occasionally spoke of his grandchildren, having a little job or helping other guests with problems. Alfred became a friend.

Like Walter. A winter regular, Walter was a big, burly guy, a proud New York Irishman with a white beard and booming voice. His computer skills were excellent. His knowledge of current events was endless. He would often challenge me on a subject and end up teaching me a wealth of information. He loved his New York but told of the expense of living there and his fears of living on its streets. It was too cold in the winter. So, he was like a snowbird who came south for the winter. Then, his family would send money for him to return in the summer. He often shared stories of the happenings on the streets, lack of services and mental health issues. Walter was a talker!

Like Pham. A short, frail, quiet Asian man, Pham was a weekly regular. He hardly said anything except thank you, but constantly mumbled to himself. Though technically skilled with computers, he had a visual impairment and had to get close to the screen to read. Life on the streets affected his physical and mental health terribly. He was often unclean with frequent sunburns, skin infections, dental decay, and a seemingly unending battle with demons.

Like Anne. A lovely woman who had a passion and talent for art, Anne was gentle, shy and private. Her attire was always eclectic, and her suitcase was organized meticulously with art materials and personal possessions. It took a very long time to win her trust. She really wasn't interested in computers, but would come into the room to see me, quietly chat, and show me her recent works. I truly missed our friendship when she stopped coming to the center.

These people will forever stand out to us. Although our journeys were so different, we were "friends" on all those Monday mornings we spent together.

# Bobby, the True Giver

By Vicki Judice

*Remarks at the 2020 Interfaith Memorial Service for the Homeless*

I am often asked how I remain hopeful in the face of so much sadness and suffering that I encounter at the Rebuild Center, especially with the knowledge that the average age of death for someone living on the street is just 50 years. One reason I remain hopeful is because I know that many lives have been saved and continue to be saved through the hard work of many in this community, who have helped hundreds move off the streets into housing. Homelessness can be ended!

That is the big picture. I am also lifted daily by the individual, selfless acts of those who are still unhoused or recently housed who still make time to help others.

I recently learned about the real meaning of selflessness on, of all days, Giving Tuesday. This is a day when many administrators in the nonprofit world are frantically contacting our supporters on Facebook, Instagram, email - you name it, every place we can think of - to give a donation to support our good work.

On the very same day that I was encouraging everyone to donate for Giving Tuesday, I learned about true selflessness, and it didn't come from any of our financial supporters. It came from Bobby, one of our guests who had recently moved into housing after living in his van for close to two years. Bobby strode into the center, glowing with a peaceful, positive energy, delivering a bike that he had purchased for one of the other guests who needed one. He didn't know anything at all about Giving Tuesday. He was just doing what he felt he could do and should do to help the world be a better place, just like you and I try to do. Bobby taught me the meaning of being a True Giver on Giving Tuesday, despite one's riches or housing status.

What Bobby wanted me to share with you tonight is that while homeless, there were plenty of reasons to give up hope. He had been working in South Carolina when his company suddenly shut down. He had trouble finding another job. He ended up living in his van which was repeatedly vandalized. His savings quickly ran out. Eventually, he found his way back to New Orleans, with everything he had left inside his van.

Bobby was intent on not letting his difficult situation determine his mindset. He channeled his experiences to be positive until his self-motivation began to reflect on other guests around him. He didn't give up on his passions or his dreams.

Recently, Bobby received the keys to his new place. "I got on my knees and thanked God for allowing me to endure." Then the unthinkable happened. On his way to his new apartment, most of his possessions fell out of the back of his van. Yet he did not despair. Bobby said, "The Holy Spirit spoke to me and said, 'What's more important? Getting the key to your own residence or worrying about a few material things you can replace?'

My faith in God allows me to believe that others needed my stuff more. I feel like I 'donated' the possessions that fell out of my van to those who might have needed them more. That's when I realized God was saying 'out with the old and in with the new.'"

Taking this idea to heart, Bobby has also taken the initiative to bring donations to the center whenever he is able. He enjoys giving what he can to help those in the same situation he was in just only a short time ago.

# I Tried to Told Ya

By Juston Winfield a.k.a Art By Jaw

*Remarks at the 2018 Interfaith Memorial Service for the Homeless*

I, Juston Winfield, was homeless for four years. During that time, the Rebuild Center opened its doors to me with loving arms. They made services available to me and those who were less fortunate as far as medical, legal, hygienic, and arts and crafts.

We take this moment to remember those who passed away due to exposure to the elements, to the weather. I was one of those people who didn't feel comfortable staying in shelters. I stayed under the Pontchartrain Expressway. I stayed at Julia and N. Tonti Streets. I never went into shelters, even on freeze nights. I just put a blanket over my tent and had a baking pan inside with candles lit to keep me warm.

One of the obstacles that homeless people face with going into a shelter is the fear that the documentation one accumulated on the streets would be lost or stolen, and the fear that they might have to start the process all over again.

I would encourage the wealthier class of people not to treat homeless people badly or disrespectfully because (Facebook quote) **"We are the same. You could be one hospital bill away from homelessness."**

The Rebuild Center helped me to start a career with art. I was encouraged to go forward. I recently purchased an artist permit and I sell art now. I have been housed.

I still go to the Rebuild Center to see those faces that were there for me when I had nothing. Those faces I call the "Grace Faces."

As Art By Jaw would say, "I tried to told ya but you didn't want heard me"!

## Martin
### By Sr. Kathleen Driscoll

*Do not judge my appearances,*
*A rich heart may be under a poor coat.*
*-Scottish Proverb*

The poverty of being unwanted, unloved, and uncared for is the greatest poverty of our day.

In 2013, Martin appeared at the Rebuild Center in New Orleans. He had been living on the street for well over several years. He was dirty and his hair and beard were long and knotted. He sat quietly on the bench away from other guests, talking to no one, asking for nothing, just watching. If you were not observant, you could just pass by Martin, as he seemed to fade into the background.

I was running a housing program for Depaul USA at the time. One day, I was moved to ask Martin if I could sit down next to him. He replied, "yes," and we struck up a conversation. I learned Martin had, at one time, held down some good factory jobs and earned good money. Over time, his mental health issues got the best of him, and he ended up on the streets in Alabama before he moved around and ended up in New Orleans. He had no income, no benefits, no food stamps, and no health insurance. It was just Martin and his few precious belongings.

During our daily conversations, I realized that I had been looking into the eyes of a homeless man and seeing the face of God.

After Martin and I developed a trusting relationship, I asked if he would like to be housed. For the first time, Martin smiled and said "yes," but that he did not have any money and could not afford rent. I reassured Martin that we would help him find a place and pay the rent until he was back on his feet. I asked Martin to come back the next day and we would begin the paperwork and start looking for an apartment.

When Martin returned, there had been a miraculous change in his appearance. He was clean, his hair was cut, and his beard was gone. I almost didn't recognize him. Over the next month, we found Martin an apartment and applied for food stamps and Social Security benefits. Martin has been successfully housed since June of 2013.

Martin and I are still in contact. He calls every month to let me know he has paid his portion of the rent. Sometimes he just calls to see how I am and sometimes he calls because the voices in his head are too much for him to handle and he needs a trusted friend to talk with. Martin's friendship is a blessing in my life.

I believe that if more people got to know those living on the margins of society, they would see them more as their brothers and sisters. They've had some really bad knocks, but they are just like us. They are loving. They are welcoming. They are helpful. They are really good people who have just had some bad luck in their lives.

# Carlton
## By Vicki Judice

His name was Carlton. He was my father, and he would have been 88 years old that wintry day in 2017. My father was a humble, generous man who taught me so much, including the importance of caring for others who were in need.

That day, some 21 years after his death, I met another Carlton at the Rebuild Center. This Carlton was cold and literally dripping wet, shivering on a stormy day when the temperature was dropping fast.

Carlton told me that he was living underneath the bridge and was reluctant to go into the overnight shelters because he could not bring all his belongings with him. He was afraid his things might be stolen.

We were concerned that Carlton would freeze to death if he didn't seek shelter that night. But he remained adamant not to go. So, we did the next best thing for Carlton, which was to load him up with new warm clothing, socks, gloves, scarves, hat, coat, and a backpack. We could do this because of the generosity of our donors who have collected these warm items for distribution.

We dried his wet clothes in our dryers. He promised to come back on Monday to talk to Kip about getting into permanent housing.

Before he parted to face the cold night ahead, I told him that my father's name was Carlton, too, and that, coincidentally, it was his birthday today.

He smiled and said that Carlton is an unusual name, seldom heard, but we agreed that it is a good and dignified name. Carlton thanked me for my help, gave me a hug, and told me he loved me.

Just like my father used to do so long ago.

# Too Blessed to be Depressed
### By Sr. Vera Butler

Each day at Lantern Light, we met and greeted people from all walks of life. All had very interesting stories and experiences. Many had faced difficult challenges yet faced each day with a smile and a feeling, "I'm blessed."

One day, a guest said, "I'm too blessed to be depressed."

I will never forget a hot summer's day when we had a volunteer group who liked to prepare and serve Saturday lunch. That meal was the only service we offered on Saturday. After the meal, I went to the office to catch up on some office work. I happened to look out the window and saw one of our guests sitting in the blazing hot summer sun. I knew Albert suffered from high blood pressure and diabetes with many underlying medical conditions.

So, I went outside and chatted with him for a little while, then asked, "Are you waiting for something?" I was amazed by his answer, "I am just waiting until you leave as I want to make sure you are safe."

This was very humbling and made me aware how caring Albert was. I assured him I was fine, but felt he was not going to leave until I did, so I gave him a bottle of water and we both left for the day.

# More Alike Than Different
## By Paisleigh Kelley

A recent transplant from Houston, Jay was excited to turn over a new leaf in New Orleans following his divorce. He'd lined up a job at a factory on the West Bank and was staying with family and friends when the COVID-19 pandemic hit. Having only been on the payroll for a few days, Jay found himself unable to pay rent, ineligible for unemployment benefits, and facing life on the streets.

I met Jay soon after the Rebuild Center's reopening, following Gov. Edwards' Stay-at-Home mandate. At that point, Jay had been homeless for nearly six weeks. He'd already gained a reputation for being helpful and considerate with our partners at Lantern Light, offering to help pick up trash after meal service. He'd also taken up residence next to Ms. L, a sweet-as-can-be elderly woman with mental health challenges who'd been sleeping out front of the center for some time. Jay felt she could be a target of theft or violence if left unaided, so he made it his duty to protect her during those long and noisy nights near the Claiborne overpass.

Our first conversation occurred when I was writing a piece on how tropical storms and hurricanes impact the unhoused community and Jay volunteered to be interviewed. We talked about Katrina, about a relative who had axed his way out of his attic to escape the rising waters and about how his nephews remain scared of thunder all these years later.

His story was powerful to listen to, but equally moving to me was the way Jay talked about the importance of hope, kindness, compassion, faith, family, and God.

"The only thing I have is God and my mama." Jay said, "That's really all I need because God sees the contents of my heart. He sees that I eat spiritually to get fit physically so that I can better care for myself and others. Sometimes it's hard and I get down on myself and my situation, but my mama reminds me that I can be the person I need for myself and trust that God will do the rest."

I was impressed by Jay's ability to be so self-assured while facing so many financial hurdles and other challenges. It didn't appear that Jay was naïve or arrogant; rather, he was sure that the experience of homelessness was merely part of his life path and that he would eventually get to the other side of it.

Jay and I established an easy rapport, and as time went on, our daily check-ins grew to incorporate topics of life beyond the center. I'd lend him books and he'd recommend music. We'd talk about our families, his son's rapping career, our personal hopes and dreams, how addiction touched each of our lives, his incarceration, and our love for New Orleans.

One morning in October, Jay arrived at the center after a particularly difficult night. Hurricane Zeta had forced him away from his sleep spot and into an overnight shelter. He arrived for shower service distraught because his ID had been stolen and he had worried about Ms. L, whom he hadn't seen for two days.

Though he was upset about having to replace his ID, he kept smiling and looking down at a ceramic, Snoopy-shaped piggybank. He told me that his mom nicknamed him Snoopy as a kid and that this glass bank was sitting in his normal sleeping spot next to Ms. L, mysteriously unscathed from the rough winds and rains from the night before. "If this little thing can make it through a night like that, then I'm gonna be just fine." he said. He asked if I'd keep Snoopy safe in my office and, for the next few months, whenever Jay had an extra dollar, he'd ask me to put it in his bank.

One morning during the holiday season, I got a phone call from my mom telling me that my father was in the ICU. COVID-19 was still rampant and traveling home to Tennessee was not an option. I went to work and struggled to put away my worry, but it nagged at me. I decided to take a walk around the parking lot and try to clear my mind. Jay approached me, elated, "What's going on, sister?" he chimed. He was about to launch into a story about his night but stopped when he saw my face and noticed my concern. He asked if he could join me on my walk around the lot.

My dad's declining health had been a topic of our conversation before because Jay and my dad shared similar maladies. I confided about how helpless it sometimes felt to know that there was nothing I could do to help and how scared I was that I might never see him again. Jay teared up. He said he understood and that, though there was little he could do, he offered to help carry some of the burden. We walked around the parking lot in silence, and, with each step, we prayed for and envisioned my dad's recovery.

In this and so many other moments, I was reminded that the barriers that divide people like myself from Jay (housing, financial security, race, class) are invisible when it comes to the power and resiliency of the human spirit.

As we entered the new year, I saw less and less of Jay. His relatives on the West Bank had stepped in to provide some meals and occasional lodging in exchange for childcare for his nephews and nieces. He was also picking up temporary gigs when he could. I had just been asking about him when my office line rang.

"Sister, are you sitting down? I have something to tell you," Jay said. I could hear the excitement in his voice. "They found me a house! Yes, they did, I ain't gonna be out here no more. Can you believe it?"

A wave of emotions came over me. I felt so much happiness and relief for Jay that there was nothing I could do but cry an ugly, full-body cry. I asked for his details and resolved to help him move in.

When I picked him up to take him to his new place, Jay was volunteering with our partners at Depaul USA who were also delivering furniture that afternoon. He showed me around his new studio apartment, telling me all about the art on the walls and describing the art he hoped to add to them. We talked for a long, long while. Adjusting to housing after experiencing homelessness is not as easy as it may seem. Jay had a brand-new life to design and it was all his to decide upon in this moment.

Before I left, I gave him his Snoopy bank, full of dollar bills and coins. Now it was Jay's time to tear up. Jay and I keep in touch. I email his mama from time to time with pictures of Jay in his new place. I feel incredibly grateful to have made this connection – to be blessed with the good fortune of knowing someone who embodies the principles and values I hold so dear, and I look forward to seeing all the ways in which Jay will succeed in the years to come.

# CHAPTER THREE:
# IN THE MOMENT

"There is a camaraderie, a sense of family at the Rebuild Center, a place where people can gather and feel safe."

- Gaylyn Lambert

Photo by Bernie Saul

Photo by Bernie Saul

Photo by Bernie Saul

Photos courtesy of Bernie Saul

Photo by Bernie Saul

# God Always Remembers
## By Fr. Thomas Stehlik

One day, the phone rang while I was in my office. It was a woman from New York who was in town, across the street from the church, at University Medical Center where her adult son was on life-support. She asked if I could visit her son and pray with her.

When I entered in the room, I met a very bright, articulate woman in her 60s. She was a writer. She thanked me for coming and began telling me that her son, Ben, had been a "traveler" for some years, moving from place to place throughout the United States, calling home every three or four months to keep in touch.

Only a couple of days before, he had overdosed on Canal Street, just across from the hospital and near the Rebuild Center. He was then breathing only with the help of a respirator and her prayer for him was for God's grace and peace, facing most certainly his final hours, especially after removing the breathing tube.

I felt such sadness from her, and her sorrow really weighed heavy on my heart. I couldn't imagine how it would feel to be in her place. Ben was still so young. Like me, she must have felt helpless.

As part of her prayer, she shared how grateful she was that somebody had the kindness and concern to stop when they saw her son collapse on the street and help him. "Words could never express how much I appreciate that my son was not alone in the last moments of his life," she said.

Sometimes when we see people on the street, it can be easy to forget that each one of them has a family and a unique story and is a child of God. Even despite our human struggles, each person has some loved one who everyday thinks and prays for them, wonders if they are safe, and if they'll ever hear from him or her again.

That day on Canal Street, someone remembered. Ben's mother never forgot. God always remembers. God never forgets.

# Flow
## By Vicki Judice

At various times during my tenure as director at the Harry Tompson Center, I would pause and jot down details about surprising events that caused me to reflect on the present moment, simple things in life, and going with the flow.

*Here is an excerpt from my journal relating to a day in January 2017.* Shortly after arriving to work one morning, I encountered Tom in the phone room who wanted me to talk to his mother, to reassure her that he was doing okay. He wasn't really doing okay, but I did talk to her. I told her we were looking out for Tom and helping him to take his medication. I told her that we cared for her son very much and enjoyed his good sense of humor and constant jokes. What I didn't tell her was that he had just seen our medical clinic staff for infected spider bites on his arms. I didn't tell her that Kip had to regularly wake Tom up to ensure he took his medication. Just that morning, he responded to my greeting, "How're you doing this morning?" with "Well, things are looking up. I haven't gotten beat up in two weeks."

While I was talking to his mother, Tom silently started to sob. He got back on the phone and, through the tears, told his mother he loved her and not to worry as we were his special angels, looking out for him. Tom died several months later from alcoholism and severe health conditions due to long-term life on the streets.

He was only 47.

Later that day, another guest was using the phone room. He was a tall man with a long, braided beard and many tattoos on his arms and face. A new guest, I feared he might be using the phone to make a drug deal. I went into the room to "check on things" and was surprised to hear the "drug dealer" saying, "Ok, Mom, I promise to keep in touch. I love you too." Well, that was certainly a surprise – the first of many that day, challenging my assumptions about what it was like to be unhoused and poor.

Then, on my way to the other side of the center, I was stopped by Patsy, a Julia Roberts look-alike, who wanted to share a spiritual reading with me from her women's devotional book. This day, she first asked for a cup of coffee, which I then snuck out of the staff kitchen for her. After taking a sip, she smiled broadly, and said, "It's the simple things in life, isn't it, Vicki?" Patsy had been sleeping at night in an alcove behind the church. I was amazed by her positivity.

Later, I went in search of Berengher and Becky, who were volunteering at the center that day. Becky was suffering from terminal cancer but wanted to spend as much time as possible there in her last days as the experience had been life-giving. Berengher accompanied her on each visit. I found them in the courtyard where Becky was swapping stories with Nathaniel who also had cancer. Nathaniel told Becky: "I refuse to despair as God has taken care of me all these years. I know He will continue to take care of me."

Throughout that day, wherever I walked from office to office I would be faced with requests: Excuse me ma'am, do you have a comb? How do I sign up for the shower? Do you have an extra coat--pair of shoes--socks--plastic bag--umbrella--backpack?

The requests were endless. I tried to address each request or connect them with a staff person who could help, but at the same time, I was also thinking, "Can I please just make it to my office so I can work on my board report without another interruption?"

Just when I thought I might have to sprint to my office door to escape all these demands, a guest named Theo suddenly reached for my elbow, causing me to stop in my tracks. I thought, "Oh, geez, what is it now?" He implored, "Excuse me, Miss, but I believe it's time for our dance?" I let out a huge laugh, "I guess it is!"

Despite my haste, I stopped and danced and laughed and appreciated what life presented to me in that moment. I was going with the "Flow." Flow was a value I came to appreciate and strive for each day. It was only in the Flow that I could enjoy whatever and whoever came my way and appreciate the beauty of the encounter, seeing the goodness of each person no matter their appearance, smell, mental state, or request.

At the end of that particular day, I sat at my desk and made a list of things to do in the next week. I looked out the window and noticed Patsy in her makeshift shelter behind the church, taking off her shoes, meticulously arranging her cardboard bedding for the evening, surrounding her little nest with a wall of suitcases to provide some security and privacy. She seemed happy, without a care in the world. I said a quick prayer for her safety that night.

Two years later, Patsy did move into a place of her own, replacing the church alcove nest for a bed in an apartment with hardwood floors. She told me that her favorite part about her new home was being able to hear the "pitter-patter" sound of her shoes on the floor.

Simple things in life indeed!

# Seafood Friday
### By Kenitha Grooms-Williams

Seafood Fridays have been a Catholic tradition in New Orleans for generations. Whether it's lunch, a night out on the town, or a quick stop before heading home, most local residents indulge in a seafood dish on Fridays.

One evening, my Friday tradition of breaking from a home cooked meal led me to a local market for dinner on the go. As I scanned the food bar, I noticed that the selection of items was quite slim and, at that moment, questioned whether it was a mistake to drive 20 minutes for a meal. Nevertheless, I began to sort through what was left on the bar when suddenly, a voice in the distance called out, "If you wait about 15 minutes, I'll have some hot fish and shrimp coming right out."

While I didn't recognize the voice, it was obvious that the man knew me. A young man, tall in stature, preceded to walk my way, greeting me with the biggest smile. He introduced himself as John and said that I had helped him years ago and he just wanted to say thank you.

Several years back, he went through a rough time and found himself homeless. He explained that he had come to the Rebuild Center for assistance and, through Lantern Light's employment services, was able to get a job and eventually regain a place of his own. John was excited to have the opportunity to express how much our help had meant to him. He would never forget the support and encouragement that led him to a better life.

As John and I spoke about his current position as the restaurant's newest head cook, I could not help but notice the gleam in his eyes and the pride in every word about his inspirational journey from losing his job and becoming homeless to successfully rebuilding his life several years later.

This unanticipated interaction with a former guest is one of the many examples of lives we have helped change at Lantern Light. John's story and the lives of so many others are continual reminders of the importance of the work we do to help those in need. While John may have experienced a temporary setback, I am glad that our dedication and support served as a motivation for him as he continues on his journey of life.

# You Can and You Do
By Emily Bussen Wain

It's 12:35 pm. I am looking forward to finally sitting at my desk and eating my turkey and cheese sandwich before lunch duty in 15 minutes.

I am a little extra tired because we were short-handed today and I had to do double-duty with the shower services. I wanted to run to the back really quick to grab some more cough drops to put in a goodie bag for a guest, Sam, who was hopping on the train the next day. He has asked for cough drops many times over the past several months as well as Chapstick every now and then. We wanted to put together a little farewell gift. Sam has been such a joy to see every day, but we are all happy he is finally going to Colorado to live with his brother.

As I am making my way to my office, I get stopped by Donald. He asked if I have a glucometer in my office, but I do not. All I can think about is sitting down and eating my sandwich. As awful as it sounds, I was tempted to tell him to see me after lunch.

I decide I can take him over to the medical office because I know there is a machine there. He checks his sugar. It was a little high, but not bad. I gave him a bottle of water and told him to drink it.

We left the medical office and Donald said: "Everybody always tells me I can't, I can't. Well, you can and you do. Thank you."

This is coming from a 6'3" 280-pound man who is not known for giving compliments. I tell him, thank you.

Moments like that are what keep me going, day in and day out. People like Donald are what make every minute here at the Harry Tompson Center so rewarding.

## The Art Lady
### By Gaylyn Lambert

For several years, I have been a twice-a-week volunteer for Lantern Light at the Rebuild Center as "The Art Lady." I set up tables on the deck where the guests can sit to draw, paint, and color for the 90 minutes I am there. Some of the guests are quite talented, but most just enjoy creating something that is uniquely their own. The guests have the option of taking their completed item with them or allowing us to hang it on clotheslines strung across the deck. Sometimes, when guests get apartments, they will take their items to display in their new homes.

Sr. Vera Butler once said that when you're homeless, you must adhere to the program where you are participating. That is, if the shelter is serving beans today, then you must eat beans. If you need to see the doctor and she only comes on Friday, then you must come on Friday, but not with the art program. The guests can do whatever they want and create an expression of whatever they are feeling that day.

One of our guests, Damien, is truly an artist. A board member was so impressed with his talent, he commissioned him to do a painting for his granddaughter's Christmas present. Another guest, Joe, who now has his own apartment, takes home copies of pages from our coloring books, and brings the finished pages back to Lantern Light to share with others or to display on the walls of our deck.

With funds provided to me by Lantern Light, I bring various craft items for the guests to use, such as coloring books, paints, drawing paper, or seasonal items for Valentine's Day, Easter, Halloween, as well as pinecones that the guests paint as Christmas trees using Mardi Gras beads for the ornaments.

I am so inspired by the attitude of our guests. Some struggle with mental issues or addictions, but for the most part, they are pleasant and grateful for the time they spend creating at the art tables. Even some of those who now have their own apartments come back daily. There is a camaraderie, a sense of family at the Rebuild Center, a place where people can gather and feel safe.

I am honored to be a volunteer at the Rebuild Center. I always leave happier than when I arrived.

# I Remember
By Sr. Anna Raimon

Venerable Nano Nagle, the foundress of the Sisters of the Presentation of the Blessed Virgin Mary, made the motto of the Nagle Family, "Deeds Not Words," her own personal motto and that of the Presentation Sisters. This motto continues to be lived throughout the world by Presentation Sisters, Presentation Associates and all Presentation People.

Venerable Nano is also known as the Lady of the Lantern. The light from Nano's lantern shines brightly at the Lantern Light Ministry in New Orleans. Nano's motto and lantern light are realized in the ministries by staff, volunteers, and guests.

I remember the day when a volunteer interviewed one of the guests and then typed up his resume. This guest came out of the office with a big smile on his face, proudly showing me his resume saying, "This is my life."

I remember the day when a staff member made homemade turkey soup for the guests. "This soup tastes just like my mom's," remarked a guest.

I remember the day when an elderly guest came into my office in need of financial assistance for his monthly rent. This guest, as I observed, was also in need of warm gloves, his hands were shaking from the cold. As I gave him my own gloves, the expression on his face communicated appreciation and gratitude.

I remember the day, while volunteers emptied bags donated for the food pantry, and at the bottom of one bag was one quarter, a true example of "the widow's mite," a small contribution that is willingly given and all one can afford.

I remember the many days when guests volunteered to empty rubbish barrels, pick up debris outside the center property, and carry in boxes of food items for the pantry. Nano's "deeds" were exemplified by each of these guests.

Love does such things.

I remember the days when staff, volunteers, and guests assembled in the courtyard for prayer and sharing of memories in remembrance of guests who had recently passed away. The prayer and reflections by those present were heartwarming, touching, and sincere. May the souls of our beloved guests rest in peace. Amen.

I remember...

I remember...

I remember...

# Mr. Johnson
By Kenitha Grooms-Williams

Mr. Johnson was 76 years old and had a difficult time obtaining a Louisiana ID card. He grew up during a time when you could go to school, get a job, and even get married without much identification. Unfortunately, Mr. Johnson relocated to New Orleans, fell on hard times, and was trying to regain some stability through a housing program. He met most of the criteria, but still needed a current state identification card.

As I asked the usual questions regarding official documents he might have to prove his identity, Mr. Johnson informed me that he had never had a copy of his birth certificate and didn't know if one even existed. When I asked about his birthplace, he explained that his mother resided on a plantation during his birth and did not have the option of going to a hospital. As a result, there was no official record of his birth. For a moment, we thought that it might be impossible to obtain this important document.

Research and a few phone calls to individuals who had a little more experience in obtaining legal documents led me to the Social Security office. Through this agency, Mr. Johnson was able to apply for a Numident record, which provided evidence of his family history and enabled him to receive a Social Security card. These documents, along with certified copies of his children's' birth certificates and a marriage license eventually assisted us in getting a birth certificate created for Mr. Johnson and, ultimately, a Louisiana state identification card.

Mr. Johnson was truly grateful that he was able to get an ID and eventually become housed. I was thankful for the wealth of knowledge and experiences he shared about his life, starting with his birth on a Mississippi plantation to the present where he faced a harsh life on the streets of New Orleans.

The fact that he was experiencing homelessness never defined who he truly was, as he understood that homelessness is only a temporary situation. He educated me about so many things as a man, an African American and an elder. I will never forget Mr. Johnson's warm personality and pray that he is safe, settled, and still housed.

# Tiny
## By Bill Kroetz

I had grown to look forward to Friday afternoons when I would arrive at the Rebuild Center to volunteer with the phone services and visit with the few remaining guests who would be hanging around the center until it closed at 2:30 p.m. Most of the guests departed right after lunch, leaving to ensure they would secure a place at an overnight shelter or found a safe place to sleep that night. But some of them hung around a bit longer, stopping in to chat with me or use the phone or the restroom one more time before closing.

One of the guests, who I got to know over the four years volunteering, was nicknamed Tiny. Believe me, his name is misleading as Tiny was anything but small. He was a very large, scruffy man, probably in his 40's, who had been sleeping outside for several years.

Many professionals had attempted to help move him off the streets, but their attempts were thwarted by Tiny's aversion to living indoors and his fear that someone might break into the house to rob him.

His possessions were few, but he did have one that was rather peculiar. It was a huge 4-foot-round cloth bag that he carried on his shoulder like Santa Claus. It contained a great deal of clothing, jugs of water, and other items. The bag seemed to grow heavier each week.

One afternoon, I decided to ask him about the bag and its contents. "Oh, that's to help me exercise. I use the water jugs instead of barbells. They and the heavy bag I carry around helps to keep me in good shape."

Despite his challenging circumstances, Tiny was always cheerful, had a great sense of humor and always shared interesting reflections on the state of the world, remarking about how things could always get better. I often heard him say, "Take it one day at a time;" "Tomorrow is another day;" and "Who knows....maybe I'll even win the lottery!"

Tiny always added joy to my day.

## Amazing Grace
By Emily Bussen Wain

It was Friday morning at the Harry Tompson Center. Things were bustling outside, and I had just sat back down at my desk. I'm not sure if it was because the song was "Amazing Grace," which I have always loved, or because Ms. R was happily singing, compared to many days, when she was upset and yelling. Or maybe it was the fact it was finally Friday after a long week.

I am sure it was a combination of all the above, but as I sat in my office, listening to Ms. R belt out "Amazing Grace," a feeling of pure joy rushed over my body. I was reminded of hearing people refer to the center as holy ground. Indeed, it is. Sure, there are plenty of difficult moments, but there are also so many memories of pure joy. And this was one of them.

It is something intangible and incredibly difficult to put into words. If you have spent some time at the center, then you get it. The Rebuild Center is a truly special place. Moments of pure joy happen daily, and they can take many forms.

Sometimes it might be something big such as a guest finally signing a lease and getting a key to their new apartment. Other times, it might be finding a book by a guest's favorite author that they told you about earlier that week. It could be having a great conversation with someone who is usually more reserved and who is allowing you the opportunity to learn more of their story.

Or it might just be hearing a beautiful rendition of "Amazing Grace."

# CHAPTER FOUR:
# ACCOMPANIMENT

*"The experience taught me that you never know what stories people have to tell unless you take the time to hear them."*
*-Gina Fulton*

Photos by Bernie Saul

Photo by Bernie Saul

## Gloria
### By Geri Kolwe and Carolyn Nee

Wednesday is our regular day to volunteer at the Harry Tompson Center and that was when we met Gloria in 2010. Right away, we could tell how friendly she was and how much she cared about her appearance, as she was always well dressed and groomed. You would never have guessed she was homeless.

Gloria knew about the center when it was located on Baronne Street before Hurricane Katrina. Gloria lost her job after the storm. Then, when her rent doubled, her whole life as she knew it was gone. Before the storm, she made small talk with the center's director whenever she happened to run into him. Now, with her life turned upside down, she would soon need his agency's services.

One day, post-Katrina, she decided to venture over to the new center and scout it out for herself and her friends. She reported back to her friends on the street that everyone at the center was so nice, so helpful, and most importantly, nonjudgmental. So, we would often see her with her friends there. Whenever they were too timid to ask for something, Gloria stepped up – a razor for Marty or socks for Angelo.

One Wednesday, Gloria was there but she was not her usual, cheerful self. She was in a bad way. When we asked her about it, she told us, "I can't take it anymore. I've got to get off the street." For the first time, we saw her despair. We knew that paperwork had been started to house Gloria, so we immediately went to work to find out the status. We located our former Jesuit volunteer Sarah, who had been working on Gloria's housing. We told her how distraught Gloria was and, lo and behold, our prayer was answered. Sarah had been trying to locate Gloria that very same week to give her the good news: she had been approved for subsidized housing. We immediately told Gloria and shared tears of joy. After securing all the basics that she needed for her apartment on Simon Bolivar, we moved her in.

Fast-forward to 2020 --- We continue to see Gloria on a regular basis. She now lives in a spacious efficiency on Esplanade Avenue where she feels very safe and comfortable in her home. She has experienced some health decline and has a condition that affects her balance and speech. The balance issues have resulted in her using a wheelchair. Her apartment is designed for wheelchair accessibility, and she is quite proficient at operating it. She remains her friendly self and can talk your arm off! Gloria likes to say, "If you can laugh at yourself, you can laugh at anything!"

About the same age, mid-60's, our memories of growing up are similar to Gloria's, who is a NOLA native and a graduate from a local Catholic high school. We can and do talk about 70's music and fashion, as well as past Mardi Gras and Jazz Fests. Gloria experienced it all. She loved strolling through the French Quarter, enjoying good New Orleans cuisine. We have a lot to talk about. We bring Gloria groceries and have some delivered. Her sweet tooth is like none we have ever seen before!

Now, her finances are stable with SSI and SSDI. Recently she gave a donation to purchase items for the Depaul housing initiative. She also donates to various causes that are dear to her, including the center and our local Catholic TV station. Pre-COVID, we took her out to lunch and shopping. Hopefully, those days will soon return.

Gloria knows and asks about our children and grandchildren. She loves it when we share pictures of them. We love our friend Gloria, whose friendship has taught us that bad things can happen to the best of people. We will never look at homelessness the same after meeting Gloria.

# Palmiro
## By Jorge Arzuaga

My name is Jorge. His name is Palmiro. We are the same age, but our upbringing and adult lives could not have been more different.

I was born and grew up in a posh and traditional neighborhood in the outskirts of Buenos Aires, Argentina's capital. My mother, of English descent, was a housewife. My father was an engineer and worked for Dupont de Demours. I attended the most prestigious English high school in Argentina. I have a master's degree in economics and business administration. I then moved on to become an industrial engineer, got married, and had three children. For 30 years, I was a banker. In 2011, I moved to Switzerland and became a senior financial advisor. I had a sophisticated life, full of material luxury.

Palmiro was born and grew up in a shantytown in northern Honduras. He never knew his father. He had more than 10 siblings, from at least five different fathers. He stopped going to school when he was 9 years old. He hardly knew how to read or write. He did what most people do in his situation to survive. Because his mother did not want him around her, he worked in the fields. He took any job he could find - building houses, gardening, and washing dishes. At the age of 22, he had his first child. Four more children would come later. But, unlike his mother, these five boys (now men), had the same parents.

In 1995, Palmiro left Honduras and came to the United States to work and send money home. It took him more than three months to travel through Guatemala and Mexico to cross the Rio Grande and reach American soil. His life here was far from what he expected. He had lots of jobs but no happiness. He travelled through many cities and in 2014, while living in Ohio, he was beaten by some men who wanted his money: 30 dollars.

After a few months, because of the beating, he started to lose sight in his right eye as well as his hearing on the same side. He could hardly work. Money ran out and he became homeless. Since winters are extremely hard in the North, he moved from Washington D.C. to New Orleans at the end of 2015.

For very different reasons, I was also in Washington D.C. during the same time. While Palmiro was living in a tent and being fed at Miriam's Kitchen, the Rebuild Center's equivalent in D.C., I was staying at one of the city's best hotels. We only had one thing in common: we were both very sad and very lonely. We both prayed for something good to happen to us. And as Palmiro came to New Orleans at the end of 2015, so did I.

We met for the first time in January of 2016 when I was volunteering at the Rebuild Center's welcome kiosk. The way he was walking towards me, his entire demeanor, the way he looked at me when he introduced himself, was striking. Sorrow and pain were written all over his body. He was very humble when he asked for my help. The kind of humility that only comes after sorrow and pain had taken over a body and soul.

I helped pay for medical procedures to repair his eyes, teeth, and right ear. He underwent five eye operations and ended up having full, removable dentures. Over the course of almost two years, I helped him a lot. And he helped me in many ways. We became friends. God has His way of making things happen.

"I believe that it is time to go back to your country and family, Palmiro," I told him once while we were having dinner together at University Hospital. It took more than three months to convince him. Alas, he felt ashamed to return to his family as a "defeated" man. *Who said that you are a defeated man, Palmiro?*

With his knowledge and concurrence, I applied all my professional skills toward getting him a Honduran ID. I contacted a lawyer and public notary there and managed to get his papers. In the U.S., I got the Honduran Consulate to issue a safe passage, so Palmiro could board a plane back to Honduras.

In August of 2018, we both flew to Houston. I was not going to let my friend fly for the first time in his life alone. My trip stopped there. He boarded a connecting flight to San Pedro Sula, Honduras. I booked the last flight back from Houston to New Orleans. I wanted to make sure that he was safe and sound in Honduras, surrounded by his loved ones before going back.

Before boarding, Palmiro gave me a long and tight hug. We were both in tears. "I have no words to thank you for what you did for me, Jorge. You were the angel that God sent me to save my life," he said. "No, Palmiro, thank you. Because you were the angel that God sent to save mine."

When his plane finally took off, I said a prayer. God had given us both an opportunity to mend our lives. And we both took it, thanks to each other. Thank you, Palmiro.

And of course, THANK YOU, GOD.

# I Feel Like a Million Bucks!
By Eva Sohl

People without stable housing struggle each day to meet basic needs for food, hygiene, clothing, and sleep - all things that most of us take for granted. The homeless experience is a tangled web of trauma and victimization, debilitating physical and mental health conditions, substance abuse, unemployment, incarceration, and housing inequities.

Ms. D is a guest who comes to the Rebuild Center a few times a month. Each time we see her, she shares a little about the challenges she is presently facing and some of the trauma that she has endured. It is common for her to report that her possessions have been stolen. One day, she was hanging up signs for her missing dog. A few weeks later, she was mourning the loss of a friend who passed away on the streets.

One morning, we welcomed her to the center for a shower. "Good morning, Ms. D! You can head right in to shower number 10." It was a busy day in the center with lots of folks eager to shower and get their daily business started.

Suddenly, I heard Ms. D screaming from the doorway of her shower stall. As the screaming continued, I ran to attend to her and keep her and our other guests safe. She was clearly in crisis mode, triggered by some unidentified catalyst.

Our security guard rushed up to see what the problem was. Sensing that his presence might escalate her fury, I asked him to give us some space. "Ms. D is very upset, and we just need to help her calm down. Can you please go find Charles?"

This semester, we have benefited from having an intern from Holy Cross University's Counseling Program. Charles, our intern, has been a critical member of our team, helping to provide direct support to our guests, as well as training staff to integrate trauma-informed care into our approach to services.

When Charles arrived at the shower, Ms. D was still emotionally and physically in panic mode. Charles calmly approached and acknowledged her overwhelming stress. His voice was soft and calm, "Would you like to take a seat and talk with me about what's upsetting you?" Ms. D looked at him, thought for a moment, and sat down. Charles knelt down to look up at her, nodding his head to show he was actively listening. As time went on, her voice decreased to a normal level.

Charles sat with Ms. D in the doorway of the shower and listened to her unload the pain and trauma she was feeling. As she reached the end of her story, he invited her to do some breathing exercises to help calm down the body. After five minutes practicing these relaxation techniques, Ms. D said she felt safe and relaxed. They made a quick plan, that she would close the door and enjoy a moment of privacy, take a nice hot shower, and give herself some time to get collected. When she was ready, she would come out and they would chat more.

Thirty minutes later, Ms. D emerged from the shower stall. "I'm sorry for all the yelling and taking so long," she said as she transported her belongings to the bench to finish getting ready by our sinks.

"It's okay, Ms. D, we know sometimes it's easy to feel overwhelmed. Are you feeling any better?"

"Oh yes, thank you."

"Are you ready to see Charles again? Should we let him know you are out of the shower?"

"Please."

Charles joined Ms. D while she put on her shoes and applied her cosmetics. They chatted about her life, the good and the bad that she had endured. The mood was much lighter, and, at times, they were laughing. "Can I ask you a favor?" Ms. D said to Charles. Unsure what to expect, Charles replied, "Sure."

"Do you have a blow dryer? I would love to dry my hair." "I think we can make that happen," Charles affirmed as he set out in search of the appliance.

As Ms. D fixed her hair, she was not only smiling, but she was also joyful. She looked like a 15-year-old getting dressed up to go to the mall with friends.

When she finished, she walked up to the staff, "I feel so much better y'all. I feel like a million bucks!" she said, striking a pose like a fashion model. We all waved and wished her luck as she set out for the day, smiling and hopeful. She not only felt clean and revived, but also felt heard and cared for.

The Rebuild Center is more than a day shelter; it is a place to find community. We pride ourselves on our ability to attend to the needs of our guests, to invite them in, to make them feel safe, and to foster a sense that no matter what their situation, they can find a sense of belonging among people who truly care about their wellbeing.

# Earl
## By Kahlise Ward

Earl had only been in our housing program for four months before leaving this earth, but he made quite an impact. His story may not be a happy one, but I want to highlight the qualities of hope, determination, resilience, and gratitude that he shared with us during his brief journey with Depaul USA. It was a true honor to get to know Earl, his story, and walk with him during his final steps of life.

Earl was considered an "old timer" on the streets of New Orleans. He had experienced homelessness off and on for over 10 years, persevering through difficult times while searching for and embracing any gifts of joy and happiness that showed up in his life. To staff and volunteers at the Rebuild Center he was well-known and well-liked. He was also known as a good friend and companion to many homeless guests.

Earl was a New Orleans native and grew up with his mom, dad, brother, and sister. He once shared that his parents were very musical, so he was raised listening to all genres of music. He also reminisced about watching old black and white movies and westerns, loving them because they were a staple from his childhood.

I had the pleasure of meeting Earl's sister Charlotte who was a great support to him during his sickness. Earl was diagnosed with Stage 4 lung cancer just days after entering our program. He was finally housed and no longer homeless when this overwhelming news was immediately laid at his feet. Earl did not miss a beat. He kept all his doctors' appointments and tried to stay positive despite his fears.

During this time, Earl was often in and out of the emergency room because he began to have difficulty breathing. He was a man who enjoyed walking a lot. This was a good thing because he relied on walking to get where he needed. Earl was in the denial stage, but his spirits were high, and he still hoped to overcome the cancer.

His condition started making it more difficult to walk. He sometimes stayed at Charlotte's house because he was scared to be alone. One day in mid-December, Charlotte brought him to the ER. This time was different. His condition worsened, and he would remain in the hospital.

The hospital is located just across the street from the Rebuild Center so we could easily visit him. I learned that he loved hot coffee so we brought him a hot coffee with each visit. Despite his physical pain, depression, anxiety, and the irony of finally no longer being homeless, yet not living in his home, Earl was always pleasant and patient. If he was unsure or upset about what the doctors would say, he would sometimes get agitated and ornery, but was easy to cheer up. In the beginning, when his appetite was still good, we would bring him burgers and other goodies like king cake and chocolate muffins (which he always insisted on sharing). We also brought him books when we learned of his love of reading. He would say all he needed was a good book and his Bible. He also enjoyed reading the Quran.

Usually, our job tasks involve helping our clients retain their housing. But in Earl's case, our job switched to keeping his spirits high, helping him make medical and life decisions, and giving him emotional support. Many difficult decisions had to be made.

During the four months I got to work with him, I was grateful to spend that time helping support Earl emotionally through his journey of cancer. He had a difficult time accepting the fate he would meet and struggled to forgive himself for not living a "better" life. Like anyone else, Earl was looking to find solace and peace, and I believe he ultimately did.

During his last days and months, Earl laughed, cried, and mostly gave thanks for all the blessings he had experienced in his life.

# The Piano
By Gina Fulton

Cecilia had no sheet music. All the music she played on the church piano came from memory. "Hey Jude," popular and classical melodies, church hymns – she played it all. "On Eagles' Wings" was my personal favorite.

I met her in 2013 when she showed up at St. Joseph's Church to ask if it was possible to play the piano there. I told her I would check with Fr. Tom, and he said that would be okay in the afternoons. She started coming often after that. I quickly noticed that her playing was from the heart and very calming and beautiful.

Cecilia was visiting the church and playing the piano for several months before we started conversing. She spoke of demons and others persecuting her and feeling very unsafe. She was very jittery and panicky, depressed and in need of a shower and clean clothes. I really didn't know too much about Cecilia other than that she was panhandling outside the church to raise funds for herself and her pet kitten "Lizard" and that, of course, she loved playing the piano.

For many months, she just wanted to play that piano. She didn't really talk to anyone else. I was her only contact. We had many conversations after she played. Sometimes I would take care of Lizard while Cecilia was playing the piano or having lunch at the Rebuild Center.

After a while, I mentioned to Sr. Kathleen that there was a woman who might need her help. She asked if she could sit in and listen to her play.

Soon, Cecilia was opening up to her, sharing that she was sleeping outside not too far from the Rebuild Center each night with her kitten, Lizard.

After they developed a trusting relationship, Sr. Kathleen helped get her into a housing program run by Depaul USA. At first, Cecilia said she didn't need housing - things would work out for her eventually when she found a job - but after a year or more sleeping outside, Sr. Kathleen finally got her to agree to housing because Lizard needed a safe home! That was it - Cecilia wanted a good home for Lizard!

Now, she will still occasionally walk the several miles over here to play the piano. She has never asked the church for money – only to play the piano. I realized that now she doesn't speak of demons or persecution, or seem depressed, only about how Lizard really loves his new home.

It took a long while to build trust and to be comfortable with her during her constant, fearful talk of people out to get her. She's come a long way and it's a joy now to see each other.

The experience taught me that you never know what stories people have to tell unless you take the time to hear them. It taught me that it is a wonderful experience to open up to individuals who are out on the street and to those who really have no one to help them.

I realized that's what I'm called to do - what we're all called to do - to serve one another the best we can, to take the time to listen to their stories and help in whatever small way we can.

The piano was the opening, the door for Cecilia to reveal more about herself and her needs. God opens the door. I have to make a choice.

Am I going to keep the door open or close it?

## Warren and Paul
By Vicki Judice

"The first thing you have to learn if you live on the street is how to take care of your feet. This means that soft shoes will not do. Ideally you would have two pairs of well-made leather boots that you alternate every day…and fresh clean socks are a must also when you live outside." - Excerpt from Paul's Blog on "Surviving Homelessness"

Paul considered himself an expert at surviving homelessness and was full of advice for other unhoused guests at the Rebuild Center. He even published a list of resources for those living on the street and submitted various writings for the Harry Tompson Center website's blog.

Just like the legendary Paul Bunyan, this Paul had many tall tales. He told of adventures in Arizona, California, Nevada, and of owning a 25-foot sailboat cruiser which he had sailed from Cuba to Louisiana a few years back, which was now docked in Golden Meadow. If only he could retrieve his sailboat, he could end his homelessness.

I figured this to be just another one of his tall tales, but Warren believed him. Warren was a longtime Rebuild Center volunteer who had had many troubles of his own. He recently started facilitating our popular Monday afternoon Share and Support weekly sessions for guests. Paul was one of the frequent attendees in the group, and he and Warren became close buddies.

Warren was intrigued by the idea of the sailboat and wanted to help Paul retrieve it. I questioned the wisdom of this expedition since Warren had no money for gas to make the six-hour trip, but Warren was adamant. So, with a little help to purchase the gas, off they went to find Paul's long-lost sailboat.

Much to my surprise, they did find the boat! Unfortunately, it had accumulated over $600 in docking fees, so they could not tow it back to New Orleans. A goal for another time.

When I saw Warren and Paul the next day, they were both beaming and couldn't stop talking about what a great time they had on their field trip to Golden Meadow. It didn't seem to matter too much that they had come back empty-handed. What mattered to Paul was that Warren had befriended him and believed in him.

During this time, Kip was working hard to find a housing placement for Paul as his health had rapidly deteriorated and it was now life-threatening for him to be sleeping outside. Kip had compiled a "List of 27" which contained the names of persons who had been sleeping in the Rebuild Center parking lot in recent years and whom he targeted for housing placement assistance. Over the next year, Kip was successful in finding housing placements for all 27, Paul included. Unfortunately, Paul only lived for four months after moving into his apartment. Warren continued to be good friends with Paul up until his own death the next year.

# A Good Neighbor
By Katey Lantto

Joshua is always a joy to have around the Rebuild Center. He's been a guest for the last five years or so. When he comes by, he always makes sure to freshen up at the sinks as he likes to look his best. Over the years that I have grown to know him, I've come to notice and value his efforts to be polite and encouraging, despite whatever hardship he faced on the streets that day.

In some of our first conversations, he asked about my family and education. Since then, he has never forgotten to ask about when I'm moving on to be the next big anthropologist or how my mother is doing. His booming good mornings and long, drawn out goodbyes are the bookend pleasantries he loves that let him know he's a respected and valued member of our Rebuild community.

Joshua is a guarded person with an angry expression on his face most of the time, but his politeness and homemaker's spirit show his softness. He's told me how he loved being a boxing coach for kids decades ago, and I can see how that love of watching something flourish has colored many of his other interests. He loves looking through donated Home and Garden magazines, showing the best ways to spruce up your space. He has always had big dreams for the kind of garden he might be able to have one day, even before he became interested in working with me to apply for housing assistance.

Most days you can find him in a suit jacket, no matter the weather, and he isn't shy about advising everyone how to dress to look decent. He has a habit of gifting little brown bags full of magnolia petals, which is one of his favorite flowers.

Last year, after much hard work and patience from both of us, Joshua signed his lease for a small studio in Mid-City, only two blocks from my own home. During the first few months of COVID before we found the unit, we had talked a lot about expectations: what his home may look like; what a case worker might ask him when they began working with him; and what neighborhoods usually have affordable units. He was adamant about finding a house in a community environment which was safe and in a good neighborhood. He also really wanted some yard space to begin tending to his dream garden.

When we found the perfect spot and a landlord willing to work with a housing voucher, I helped him move his belongings from the City of New Orleans Shelter and Engagement Center to his new home.

Joshua had so many boxes! They filled the car to the brim, even putting some on his lap. As we drove to his apartment, he told me that all these boxes he's held onto for these last five years are full of church clothes. His first plan, once the pandemic subsided, was to establish himself at the neighborhood church and build his community through it.

It is extremely touching to have a longtime guest and friend like Joshua move into my neighborhood and reminds me that I share the responsibility to be a good neighbor.

Every person on the block and every unhoused person we pass is a neighbor, and we all need to treat them as such.

I know for myself, having Joshua down the road has helped me realize how many more neighbors I have. I am always looking for him when taking a walk so that I can introduce him to the other people I've begun to know. I brought him a poinsettia on Christmas Eve, and we are planning to go to church together, dressed to the nines, once in-person services resume.

This is how I want to build community for Joshua and for myself, and I am grateful for his reminder of the value of being a good neighbor.

# CHAPTER FIVE: GROWTH

*"My art has gone from coloring books to painting to photography to making my own style of abstract art.*

*All of this has really given me a purpose."*

-   *Louis Herrera*

# Art Opened Doors
By Louis Herrera

My name is Louis Robert Herrera. I'd like to tell you about my time at the Rebuild Center. I first met Vicki and others at the Rebuild Center eight years ago when I had been homeless for six years, struggling with mental illness. It took two years, but with the help of center staff, I was finally able to get assistance to find permanent housing. I have been off the street now for six years.

One of the first persons I met at the Rebuild Center was Sr. Dolores who asked if I would like to color on some coloring book sheets. At first, I thought, "Why would I want to do such a silly thing?" But curiosity got the best of me, and one day I thought "Why not? I don't have anything better to do." Lo and behold I started to really get into coloring on those sheets. Then I realized I wanted to also try different types of art, so I started doing some painting whenever the Art Lady set up art tables at the center. I really enjoyed it and started realizing this is something that I might be good at.

Then, when Heather started the annual New Orleans Photo Project for persons who had experienced homelessness in New Orleans, I tried my hand at that, too. Soon, I developed a passion for photography. I won several prizes over the years with this contest, and it has been an amazing experience for me.

Later, the center hosted an art show where we could sell our work. I sold many of my paintings there. Thanks to so many people at the Rebuild Center, I have started a productive life of painting and playing music, as well as learning to deal with my mental illness.

My art has gone from coloring books to painting to photography to making my own style of abstract art. All of this has really given me a purpose. My art has given me a way to express myself in a healthy way, even drawing dark art to relieve negative feelings.

I am proud of my development as an artist, but I am most proud to be a volunteer at my church. It is there each Friday that we help the homeless, and I am like their case manager. It is so very gratifying.

I have also sought professional help to deal with bipolar depression and am on medication to keep me from falling into my own dark prison. Now, I can add to my list of accomplishments, writing a story in a friend's book. I feel my life has been very successful and can't wait to see what else life has to offer me.

Whatever the future holds for me, please keep me in your prayers. Thank you and don't forget humans were made to be connected, so if you need help, please seek professional help --- God bless!

# No One Ever Asked Me About Housing Before
By Kip Barard

In the nearly three years I had worked at the Harry Tompson Center, I saw the same sight at least once a week when I arrived at work early in the morning.

Waylon, one of our regular guests, would be sleeping behind St. Joseph's Church, right underneath the back stairs in a small, 10' x 8', covered concrete space. Each morning I would try to engage him in conversation, but he was always too intoxicated to stand up, so conversation was out of question. Every time I attempted to speak with Waylon, he would try to rise, holding the wall to steady himself, but inevitably slouch or stumble back down to the ground.

Needless to say, our conversations didn't amount to very much, but I never gave up. Waylon tended to sleep just about every day until around noon and then disappear, but reappear the next morning, intoxicated once again. For years, we repeated the same pattern, though he almost never came inside the Rebuild Center for our services.

Finally, one day - the date was April 4 - I arrived at the center for work and found Waylon actually awake, standing and walking straight up without the assistance of the wall. Amazed, my first thought was, "Okay, now I can finally have a coherent conversation with him and, hopefully, he might even be interested in getting off the streets."

I asked him: "Waylon, what do you think about working with me to get into housing?" He said, "I don't know. No one ever asked me about housing before."

He agreed to come into the center where we spent the next few hours discussing his life and potential housing options. I learned that not that long ago, Waylon had been living the "good life." He actually had a college degree, although over time, alcoholism led to losing his housing. We discussed the steps we needed to take for him to obtain a place of his own. He seemed a little surprised about the whole process but agreed to work with me to achieve that goal.

It took a good bit of work and numerous days when Waylon was sober enough to complete the housing paperwork. Finally, we were able to get him into a permanent supportive housing unit at the UNITY-administered Sacred Heart Apartments where he has been living now for six weeks. Even better news! His case manager informed me recently that Waylon has done something amazing. He has been sober for ten days in a row - all of his own accord. After getting housed, Waylon decided to quit drinking.

I am proud of Waylon and my work with him. He is in a safe place now and doing well. It made me realize that anyone can become homeless - even me - and that is a scary thing.

Recently, Waylon came back to thank me and give me a hug. He was standing up just fine - without a wall to steady him - and wanted me to know that he was living the good life again.

# Elise
By Jessica Lovell

I wasn't always able to pick up the phone when Elise called, as she called several times each day, but on that day I did. I never knew what to expect as her calls often presented difficult problems for me and my staff to figure out.

Elise had been off and on the streets for several years when she entered our supportive housing program. She was a native of New Orleans and came from a large family, although many have passed on. Even while on the street and in and out of jail, she maintained contact with her older sister, Darlene, who often plays a motherly role in Elise's life, but was unable to accommodate her in her home.

For a while, Elise wouldn't spend the night in the apartment we found for her due to complications relating to mental illness. Yet, we didn't give up. With the help of a medical and mental health team who provided in-home care, we finally persuaded her to remain in her apartment.

These days, Elise is blossoming and really enjoys activities like cooking for her neighbors and learning to ride a bike. She adopted a kitty that often came to her door looking for food. After a year remaining in her apartment, she is eager to learn more about improving her life situation and helping others.

That morning when Elise called, I was preparing for the numerous tasks that lay ahead of me that day. I hoped that whatever Elise was calling about, it wouldn't be too challenging, but that day, she presented no problem at all.

Her words stunned me into silence. "Jessie, I just wanted to call and tell you that I'm listening to my prayers today and wanted to say thank you for all you do. It's a lot. I am praying that you feel the grace of God's love and blessing and have a really great day today. Thank you for always being there to help me and thank you for helping others. Keep your head up, Jessie."

I stopped in the moment, warmed by her heartfelt words, and let her blessing sink into my heart. I was feeling so grateful for Elise and her blessing.

Her call gave me much needed strength that day. My mantra for the day was, "I got this, I'm good! Elise has sent her blessings and I can handle anything!"

## Good News or Bad News
By Sr. Vera Butler

There was a young man named Robert who was 26 years of age. Robert's mother died at childbirth, so he lived with his grandmother and dropped out of college after two years. He was employed at a local restaurant where he earned minimum wage. Shortly after Hurricane Katrina, his grandmother died, and he was unable to afford rent, so he became homeless.

Robert was always jolly and upbeat. During morning sign-in, he would always give a fictional character's name. Once, I asked why he gave these names and he said that he tries to mimic that character for the day because it kept him focused. Eventually, he participated in a culinary arts program and found out he was a good cook. At one of the classes, he had to prepare a dish for 20 people. After the class, he was free to take the dish home, but brought it to the Rebuild Center to share. It was a delicious meal, but I remember feeling rather guilty eating it when I believed he never knew where he would get his next meal.

Robert eventually qualified for permanent supportive housing and moved into a place of his own. Soon after, he got a call for an interview at a seasoning factory. All went well at the interview and Robert had to have drug and health tests. When Robert returned, he said, "I have good news and I have bad news. Which do you want to hear first?" I said, "Give me the good news."

Robert proceeded to say he passed the drug test but failed the health test. His blood pressure was extremely high, which disqualified him from getting hired. However, the company did say they would hold a place for him if he could get his blood pressure under control. The center had a doctor who worked with our guests and had treated Robert in the past. The doctor asked me to pull Robert's chart and he would see him at the center at lunchtime.

We assisted Robert with his medication, but it took almost a month to get his blood pressure under control. He eventually started his job and again met many challenges. The river ferry that should have taken him close to his place of work was out of commission and the other ferry was a 45-minute walk – which he had to do on both sides of the river. Then, his shift was from 11 p.m. to 7 a.m., standing all night. His feet bothered him, and his work, unfolding boxes, was rather boring at the beginning. To make it more interesting, he put his initial on a concealed corner of the boxes!

He persevered, was promoted, and offered a 401K, which at first, he could not afford to contribute. I encouraged him to take the leap and get the 401K as the company would pay 80% when he paid 20%. He now has retirement savings.

Robert's story was indeed a success story, one with many challenges, but he kept his focus and achieved.

# Homeless Doesn't Mean Hopeless
By Kenitha Grooms-Williams

Sam's return to New Orleans was bittersweet. Although he was born and raised here, he recalled that some of his most difficult times took place in this city. Nevertheless, Sam proclaimed that his love of art and the love he received from the staff at Lantern Light and others at the Rebuild Center kept him coming back.

During Sam's adolescence, his knack for drawing and painting grew. As time went on, he rose to the ranks of an accomplished artist and his gift led him miles from his native city of New Orleans. His artwork has been displayed all over the country. He boasts that at the peak of his career, his pieces ranged from sketches of individuals visiting the French Quarter to corporate commissions, including one from The Coca Cola Company.

Though he has battled depression, addiction, and homelessness, perhaps contributing to his career demise, his faith will not allow him to quit. He is proud of what he has achieved as an artist in the past and is hopeful for what lies ahead in the future.

# Ice Cream and Burgers
By Claire Mulligan

Lanh had been a regular at the sunrise shower service at the center for many years. He was always a quiet man of few words, yet appreciative of the staff, volunteers, and a hot shower. Sometimes he was known to share an apple or even a piece of cheese from his sandwich. He does not like to waste!

Lanh suffers from mental illness. He usually appears to be in a quiet conversation with someone, yet there is no one sitting beside him. As we've gotten to know Lanh, we have also gotten to know the "voices," as he calls them. He will often ask questions on their behalf and translate the information back to the "voices." We've learned they are a part of Lanh and so we welcome them too!

Lanh shared that he became homeless after his mother died five years ago. Prior to entering our Depaul housing program, he slept outside near the Rebuild Center and would visit daily for a shower and meals. A few other agencies attempted to work with him on housing but were unsuccessful. He simply was uncomfortable with the idea of housing.

We decided the first step working with Lanh was to build trust. We spent months just talking to him about housing and what it might be like for him to live in a place of his own. When the time came, Lanh was still hesitant to even get in a car to go look at apartments. Little by little, we forged a relationship with him, hoping that our time, patience, and consistency would be rewarded.

A great apartment opened up with an amazing landlord, where we thought Lanh would be comfortable. He would have easy access to a grocery store, and he would already be familiar with the area, as it wasn't too far from his spot under the bridge and the Rebuild Center. We were elated when Lanh hesitantly agreed to sign a lease.

On the day he moved in, we first took Lanh to the grocery store to make sure he would not go hungry. He asked for ice cream, hamburgers and coke. We were humored and extremely encouraged by the specifics of his request. He would be moving into his new place with the foods of his choice.

Lanh has now been housed for six months. Each time we visit him, he has more and more to say. Soon after he was housed, he told us he "wouldn't want to be a bother but would love a radio to listen to the oldies." He hung artwork he was gifted from local students on his mantle and began to make his home his own. Aside from flipping burgers and listening to the oldies (or Toni Braxton), Lanh enjoys puzzles, anything blue, and going for walks. He remains incredibly appreciative of the Depaul team and warms our hearts each time we visit.

Lanh's story reminds us that small victories should be celebrated. Asking for ice cream and hamburgers helped empower Lanh to feel safe in his new home. We all agree that Lanh knows a good thing when he sees it…and when he tastes it!

After all, who doesn't love ice cream and burgers?

# CHAPTER SIX: RESILIENCE

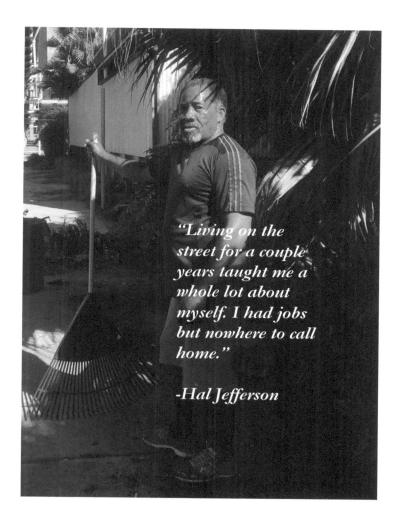

"Living on the street for a couple years taught me a whole lot about myself. I had jobs but nowhere to call home."

-Hal Jefferson

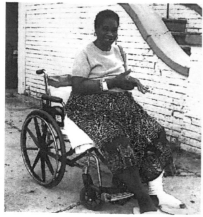

Photo courtesy of B.B. St. Roman

Photos courtesy of Bernie Saul

Photos courtesy of Bernie Saul

# Being Homeless, Having a Home.

By Hal Jefferson

*Remarks at the 2015 Interfaith Memorial Service for the Homeless*

Being homeless, sleeping under freeways, parks, empty buildings. Watching people fight over cardboard boxes and spots under the bridge as though they were paying mortgages on them, being assaulted twice myself.

My place is a five-star suite to me. No more standing in line for everything. Waiting for showers, waiting to eat, wondering if my name will be called to get in the shelters at all.

Come on man, I'm in control of it all now. Meals are great, being the good cook I am, having a clean bathroom, bed, kitchen, even a backyard to play in.

Living on the street for a couple years taught me a whole lot about myself. I had jobs, but nowhere to call home. Working and sleeping on the street is a big challenge. You cannot tell other people to be quiet "because I have to go to work tomorrow." It never works. Believe me, being homeless is not a job you go apply for.

This is just life happening, so you learn to fight for it and not squander it, living under a cloud of impending doom. You learn that life is not always fair, bad things happen to good people. You learn that the statement, "In giving, we receive," is really true.

You stop maneuvering your life as a consumer, looking for your next fix. You start distinguishing the differences between guilt and responsibility and honesty and integrity. They are not the outdated ideals of a bygone era, but the mortar that holds us together, the foundation upon which you must build your life.

I've learned to stop personalizing things. God's not punishing you or failing to answer your prayers. So, slowly you begin to take responsibility for yourself. Make a promise to the man in the mirror and make it a point to keep smiling. Trust and stay open to every wonderful possibility.

Finally, with courage in your heart and God by your side, you take a stand, a deep breath, and begin to design the life you want to live as best you can.

If you still need help, try this: love is patient, love is kind. It does not envy or boast. It is not proud. It does not dishonor others. It is not self-seeking. It is not easily angered. It keeps no record of wrongs. Love has no delight in evil but rejoices with truth. It always protects, always trusts, always perseveres.

Love never fails. Try it.  I did, thank God. Bless you all.

# Home
## By Sr. Enid Storey

One winter afternoon in 2008, I found myself sitting on one of the benches in the center, talking with a very spirited and determined woman whose name was Bessie. It was just this past year that she had begun coming to the center for lunch. Our conversation that day was unbelievable. She was able to recount so many stories from 73 years of life, but her Hurricane Katrina story is amazing.

Bessie owns her own home in Gentilly, a part of the city that was severely damaged during Katrina. Since her return to the area in early 2006, she lived in a FEMA trailer, which had to be removed because of the formaldehyde. During that time, she began the long and arduous task of making her house livable again.

At first Bessie considered herself lucky. A church group gutted her home, and she was able to finance some of the electrical repairs. She then hired a contractor to repair part of the interior of the house. He took the rest of her money, paid in advance, but did not do the work. Presently, she is pursuing legal action against him to refund the money, but nothing has come of it yet.

The other day, Bessie told me that she found someone to put down seven tiles on the bathroom floor in her gutted home. He then installed the toilet. She now has running water inside her home. She sleeps in a bed that is standing on the sub-floor. Her home is still without walls, finished floors or ceilings. The electricity is off, which translates into no lights, refrigeration, or power for a fan. Here in New Orleans, temperatures have been in the high 90's for quite a while now.

The simple things in life are important to Bessie. She has a roof over her head and a door to close. Outside is a beautiful homemade sign that says "Home." She is hopeful that a church group will repair the electrical wiring and put up the sheetrock and walls of her home.

Since Hurricane Katrina, it has been three long, rough years for some people in our city who still struggle to repair and move back into their homes. If you visit New Orleans, you will find that the French Quarter, Audubon Park and Zoo, the museums, the French Market, the Aquarium, and parts of City Park are back and looking even better. That is great.

But let's not forget the many Bessie's who are still attempting to rise out of the destruction of Katrina.

# Rebuilding Today for a Better Tomorrow
By Kenitha Grooms-Williams

Before going to prison, Jim was a young pastor who ministered to the homeless in Arkansas. For years, he was responsible for counseling individuals who were formerly incarcerated. He was also instrumental in establishing programs ensuring they had safe places to stay and opportunities that would lead to better lives. He knew that his message of redemption and restoration in Arkansas had impacted hundreds of lives, but he never thought that he would need these words of encouragement himself.

Due to an overzealous attitude and a series of bad decisions 20 years ago, Jim found himself on the wrong side of the law and was sentenced to 12 years in prison. Jim admits that the choices he made warranted his incarceration. He used his time in prison wisely and was able to further his education by receiving certificates in theology and divinity. He also had the time to reflect on where life had taken him, and what he needed to do to create a new path.

Once Jim was released from prison, he made his way to New Orleans in hopes of making a fresh start, at a time of rebuilding in a new city. Despite being homeless since relocating to New Orleans, he made great strides in getting his life back on track. Through Lantern Light, he was able to get proper identification, apply for various jobs and learn about a local culinary program he completed.

Jim is thankful for the continual opportunities to minister to people traveling down the same path. He believes that "by continuing down this straight and narrow path, I will receive the promises and rewards for being obedient to my Creator."

166

# Liz and Lessons Learned
By B.B. St. Roman

Of the 10,000+ homeless persons I have assisted since 2004, one reached the very top of my "most challenging" list and at the same time reached the very depths of my heart.

Liz and I could not have been more different. She was a very large woman with severe mental illness who thought nothing of letting diarrhea run down her legs inside her dress to form a big brown puddle on the sidewalk. WOW! I was immediately fascinated. You see, when I first met her, I'd only been a year into my job and was still very green regarding assisting homeless persons. Over the course of the next six years, Liz single-handedly taught me all I needed to know.

**The first lesson she taught me was how important it is to have a sense of humor.** How could I not smile when the police called me on the radio to remove her and her poop from the sidewalk of a Canal Street business? By the time I got there, she was dashing five blocks away with four police officers chasing after her to try to hold her in place for me! How could it not warm my heart when she then saw my van and rushed to get inside?!

**The second lesson I learned was to always show respect and take seriously what someone has to say.** Liz taught me this a week or so after Katrina hit, when I came upon her waiting for a bus at St. Claude and Elysian Fields. I tried to explain that RTA was no longer operating, but she insisted that a bus would come. Lo and behold, an RTA bus suddenly appeared, so she flagged it down, hopped inside and off they went. Little did she know that it was full of National Guard soldiers - and little did they know that she had a huge brown stain on the back of her dress! To this day, I wonder who ended up more surprised.

A few months later, when she returned to New Orleans after evacuating from Katrina, Liz taught me **my third lesson: How to be resourceful and navigate the system from scratch.** At that time, there were no case managers around to take on her situation and find her housing, so I had to learn every step of how to obtain a state ID, birth certificate, Social Security card, disability income, food stamps and, finally, a Housing Authority of New Orleans voucher. However, before we could go to each of those offices, she first needed to shower and put on fresh clothes. Once, when I had run out of options to get her a shower at a shelter, I ended up holding a sheet around her as she bathed at a spigot in an alley in the French Quarter! Luckily the resourcefulness paid off, as soon thereafter we were out choosing an apartment and getting furniture, groceries, clothes, everything she needed. What a wonderful relief!

Little by little, I found out Liz had family and four children. Liz's mental illness had driven her away from them when she was still a young mother, and they never forgave her for leaving. Seeing how much pain this caused on both sides, **I learned a fourth lesson: How to accept and appreciate mental illness.** I had to be able to roll with her delusions. When I came upon her sitting out in the sunshine, talking away, I asked her politely whom she was talking to. She replied, "God."

Over the years filled with so many intense adventures, Liz taught me **my fifth and most important lesson: Have patience and compassion at all times.** It is with that spirit that we could accomplish so much together and enjoy true friendship. We trusted one another; we were always happy to see each other; we would have fun together no matter what we did, whether it was going on a simple grocery run or cleaning up the messes she made in her apartment.

Over the next few years, Liz was in and out of housing. It was during these times that I occasionally took her to the Rebuild Center to clean up, take a shower, or to obtain an ID card.

Eventually her health deteriorated, and Liz moved to an assisted living center, so others took over her care. However, that did not end our friendship.

On one of my many visits to her, she told me about a dream she had about me, which she summed up as a fight between good and evil. In the dream, an evil witch was trying to stab Liz with a sword. Suddenly, I appeared as the good warrior, also with a sword in hand. I whispered some secret words in her ear about how to protect herself, and when she turned to the witch again, the witch had lost her sword. Liz said that after she woke up, she knew I was protecting her and that she would always listen to me.

Like virtually all the homeless persons I have assisted over the years, Liz made me realize how much we were really sharing a level field. We gave back and forth; we helped and taught each other at the same time; we recognized the good in each other. In this way we created a pleasant and positive balance, making it easy to look back and smile at all the memorable moments we shared and will always treasure.

# Danny

By Jessica Lovell

Danny's experience with homelessness began five years ago. Here are bits and pieces of his story, starting when he was around 25 years old.

A fun story he shared with me tells of a time in the 1980's when he hitchhiked to the Grand Canyon from Cedar Rapids, Iowa. Danny made a sign that said, "I have a driver's license." Clever, he is. He was first picked up by a guy who sold shovels out of the back of his truck and liked to drink. Danny drove. One night, they camped on the side of the road somewhere in Colorado and woke up to the most beautiful scenery of Pike's Peak.

Danny also hitchhiked and rode a few hundred miles with a police officer. He met the officer under an overpass in the middle of a sandstorm, where people had gathered to wait out the storm. When they reached the Grand Canyon, Danny thanked the officer and then hiked from the top to the bottom where he slept by the river. He spent a few days exploring and admiring the beauty of the Grand Canyon and remembers that experience as one of his fondest memories.

After many years living in different places and working in construction, he ended up in New Orleans. Danny befriended the father of a construction boss and for the next 10 years, Danny took on the role as the man's caretaker. When the older man passed away, Danny was asked to leave the house, so it could be sold. It was then that he first experienced long-term homelessness.

Although still working sporadically, he ended up being homeless off and on for several years before discovering the Rebuild Center. He began working with a case manager to meet goals that would help him be approved and referred to a supportive housing program. It was in the middle of this process that he broke and shattered his knee.

This led to multiple surgeries during which Danny was still sleeping on the street. Imagine the difficulties he faced making doctor's appointments, recovering from surgeries, healing his body, working to gather necessary documents needed to end his homelessness, among an array of other necessary tasks presented in the face of homelessness, such as securing food. At the end of the day, he would hobble to his street bed in the abandoned building where he stayed and try to get comfortable.

I remember seeing Danny around the center during those days. A long, black, orthopedic cast encased his limb from ankle to thigh. I asked about the difficulties he faced navigating the streets on foot and dealing with his pain, trying to recover. I wondered how on earth he managed to get through all those surgeries while homeless? I was impressed by his resilience, determination, and survival skills, as well as his ability to coordinate all his doctor's visits and surgeries.

He was determined, despite his painful leg injury and surgeries, to remain on the path and do everything he could to be accepted into a supportive housing program. It was a long wait, but he was finally approved and Depaul was able to accept him into our housing program. Already knowing him from the Rebuild Center, we were very excited to be able to help him with housing and move forward with any other goals.

Since coming into the program, Danny has been very positive and could not be happier to be able to embrace stability. He started trying to find work painting but has found that strenuous work causes his body immense pain. He has stayed positive and focuses his energies inward.

The other day, I visited to see how he was doing in his apartment and found him planting flowers in his front garden. He shared how he had painted his neighbors' railing and then decided to paint his, too. He was proud to show me how he had matched the color purple of his LSU cap at the hardware store for the railing. "Now I have an LSU railing!" He has plans to repaint the window trim and some of the interior of his apartment. Luckily, his landlord has been supportive, and Danny is a great painter.

My admiration for Danny has only increased. This is a man who survived homelessness while undergoing numerous painful leg surgeries yet has never complained. His perseverance and transformation of pain encourages me to be the best person I can be, a most welcome reminder I am always grateful to receive.

Now Danny is on to another episode of his life. His amazing strategic coordination skills are now being used to help beautify his neighborhood and focus on moving forward in life.

# If At First You Don't Succeed
By Kenitha Grooms-Williams

It was Friday morning, right before 9:00 a.m., and Randy was eager to see a social worker. He had been hired the previous day at a new restaurant and needed to complete an online training in order to attend the upcoming orientation. As I exited the door, Randy approached me and expressed urgency in receiving assistance. He was determined to work at an innovative, new restaurant in town and wanted to make sure he could obtain his training certificate before the orientation on Tuesday morning to solidify his completion of the course.

As I read through the sign-in sheet, I noticed that it might take some time before the social worker would call Randy's name, so I offered him the opportunity to begin the training using a computer in an unoccupied office. Randy gladly accepted and sprinted towards the door. After turning the computer on and wishing him success, I headed to the office door to give him some privacy.

Little did we know that what we both assumed would be an easy task for Randy to complete would become a two-day crash course learning computer basics. For several hours, Randy maneuvered through the online course, hitting the next and back buttons, while trying to memorize every statistic, term, and procedure for operating in the kitchen. Finally, he reached the end of the training and completed the exam in less than an hour. His enthusiasm was short-lived; his results were two points less than the passing score.

With a few days left before orientation, I encouraged Randy to retake the test. As lunch time approached on Monday, Randy anxiously repeated the training for the last time. He reviewed notes taken during the course and proceeded to take the exam one more time. With a bit of hesitation, he pressed the enter button to receive his results and surprisingly found a passing score. Randy was filled with much more than just delight. In that moment, pride oozed through every word he uttered as we printed the necessary documents needed for orientation the next day.

The success Randy achieved on that day is one that neither he nor I will ever forget. While passing the training exam enabled him to obtain a full-time job, for me it served as a reminder that, "if at first you don't succeed, try and try again."

# Onward

Thank you for taking the time to read these stories of hope and compassion from St. Joseph's Rebuild Center. Proceeds from the sale of this book will support the center's operations.

Perhaps you now have a better understanding of the implications of homelessness and poverty on a personal level. Perhaps you feel the distance lessening between you and those in need.

Perhaps you are inspired to get to know someone who is unhoused. Or perhaps, you simply want to do more, and realize there are indeed practical ways to help those in need, even if it doesn't involve too much of your time or resources.

Your participation, no matter how small, is welcomed. For more information about the Rebuild Center and its partner agencies and how you can help, drop in sometime or visit us online:
www.Harrytompsoncenter.org
www.Lanternlight.org
www.Depaulusa.org
www.Stjosephchurch-no.org

# Meet the Story Contributors

**Jorge Arzuaga** worked with banks in the United States and Switzerland for 30 years before becoming a fulltime volunteer in 2015. He became a Vincentian lay missioner with the St. Joseph parish community and has been involved in many aspects of volunteering with the Rebuild Center as kitchen worker, meals line monitor, kiosk welcomer, and bike project assistant.

**Sr. Suzanne Anglim** is a Daughter of Charity who moved to New Orleans in 2018 after living in El Paso, Texas, for many years. She has volunteered at the Rebuild Center for over three years and enjoys being a compassionate and respectful presence to those who come to sit and share with her about their lives.

**Kip Barard,** a New Orleans native, joined the Harry Tompson Center team in August of 2013. He had previously worked for 15 years in various social service agencies in the New Orleans area, including Odyssey House and ARC, helping the unhoused and other underserved populations. Previous to nonprofit work, he was a respiratory technician at Charity Hospital. As the program director, Kip provides and coordinates case management services to vulnerable guests of the Center and helps them secure housing.

Jorge Arzuaga      Sr. Suzanne Anglim.      Kip Barard

**Sr. Vera Butler** is a Presentation Sister of the Blessed Virgin Mary. Born in County Kerry, Ireland, she entered the sisters' congregation after high school. For 60 years, she has been involved with corporal works of mercy for those living on the margins of society in both Ireland and the United States. She has been an educator, a school principal, a development director, an outreach coordinator, and an executive director. For 20 years, she served as the outreach coordinator for St. Joseph's Catholic Parish in New Orleans. There, she founded Lantern Light Ministry, helped to establish the Tulane Canal Neighborhood Development Corporation and helped to establish the Rebuild Center in 2007. She received the Catholic Extension's Lumen Christi Award in 2006. She presently lives in San Antonio where she continues her "lantern works" for those in need.

Baltimore native **Sr. Kathleen Driscoll,** a Daughter of Charity, arrived in New Orleans in 2012 as the first local director of Depaul New Orleans. With offices based out of the Rebuild Center, she established two housing programs that help chronically homeless persons transition from life on the streets to dignified, independent housing. Before coming to New Orleans, Sister Kathleen was director of Catholic Charities in Gallup, New Mexico for six years where she worked with a population that included seven different tribes of Native Americans. She presently lives in St. Louis where she works in social services administered by the Daughters of Charities.

Sr. Vera Butler          Sr. Kathleen Driscoll

**Bernadine Dupre,** a New Orleanian, worked with the State of Louisiana Department of Labor for 48 years before retiring and becoming a Vincentian Lay Missioner with St. Joseph's Church and a volunteer at the Rebuild Center. She first started volunteering with kitchen duties and then added weekly shower monitoring. She is a member of the Harry Tompson Center's Gala Committee.

**Liam Fitzgerald** started volunteering at the Harry Tompson Center when he was just 15 years old while a student at Jesuit High School in New Orleans. His involvement with the center evolved into employment as a center assistant from 2015 to 2018. He has also worked as a resident advisor with the City of New Orleans Shelter and Engagement Center, and more recently, as an outreach worker with Travelers Aid Society New Orleans.

**Gina Fulton** arrived in New Orleans via Pittsburgh in 1983 to work with a river transportation company where she was employed for 25 years. She then served as the church receptionist for Immaculate Conception Parish for several years and then with St. Joseph's Parish where she has served as the church receptionist since 2010.

Bernadine Dupre          Liam Fitzgerald          Gina Fulton

A native New Orleanian, **Kenitha Grooms-Williams, LMSW**, began volunteering with Lantern Light Ministry in 2009 after meeting Sr. Enid Storey at St. Peter Claver Church. She volunteered with Lantern Light while working on her master's degree in social work after leaving a 10-year career in advertising and public relations. Kenitha has been the executive director of Lantern Light Ministry since 2015.

**Louis Robert Herrera** was born in Santa Fe Springs, Calif., but makes his home in New Orleans these days. An artist, musician, church volunteer and writer, his life as an artist is continually evolving.

**Hal Jefferson** was born in Mississippi but has lived in New Orleans for many years. He gave the testimony for the New Orleans Archdiocesan Interfaith Memorial Service for the Homeless in 2015. Hal served on the Harry Tompson Center Advisory Council and created the Willing Workers Program which provides landscaping and other maintenance services at the Rebuild Center.

Kenitha Grooms-Williams      Louis Herrera      Hal Jefferson

**Paisleigh Kelley** is Harry Tompson Center's Communication Director. She is a graduate of the University of Tennessee and holds a master's degree in communication. She has spent the better part of her career working in education and the nonprofit world. Originally from Nashville, Paisleigh has been living in New Orleans since 2017 with her husband and their two dogs. Outside of work, you can find Paisleigh pursuing her own creative writing projects and enjoying the festivities that New Orleans has to offer.

**Geri Kolwe** and **Carolyn Nee** are longtime volunteers of the Harry Tompson Center. **Geri** grew up in Old Jefferson, attended St. Matthew Church, Dominican High School and University of New Orleans. She worked as an oil and gas accountant at Dominion Energy where she was blessed to retire at age 53. She started volunteering with HTC's phone services in 2010 and is active with the agency's annual gala fundraiser. Geri has recruited many friends to support the center and help with haircuts, phone services and donations of clothing, toiletries, and other necessary items.

**Carolyn Nee** moved to New Orleans from Florida in 1989 and worked as a geo-science technician with Dominion Energy. There, she met Geri Kolwe who invited her to volunteer at the center. She started as a phone services volunteer and later joined the gala fundraising committee. She cherishes her time at the center where so many friendships have blossomed. Carolyn is a member of St. Mary Magdalen Church and volunteers at the Audubon Zoo.

Paisleigh Kelley          Geri Kolwe and Carolyn Nee

**Bill Kroetz** has been a volunteer with the Harry Tompson Center since 2016. He is a member of St. Joseph's Parish. He retired from many years in the retail business and is a proud survivor of Hurricane Katrina.

**Gaylyn Lambert** has volunteered with Lantern Light Ministry since 2012. She started volunteering after delivering donated food from the People Program. She was so intrigued by the center's work that she asked if she could volunteer. She first started helping with Lantern Light's meal preparation and later coordinated the art program when Sister Dolores Cooney, who started the program, departed for England.

After graduating from Loyola Chicago with a B.A. in Anthropology, **Katey Lantto** served as a Jesuit Volunteer for the Harry Tompson Center in 2017-18. Following that year of service, she started working full-time as an agency case manager and coordinates the bike program. A native of Minnesota, Katey now calls New Orleans home.

Bill Kroetz        Gaylyn Lambert        Katey Lantto

A lifelong New Orleanian, **Jessica Lovell** graduated from Tulane University School of Social Work in 2015 with a Master of Social Work. While working towards her degree, she completed a yearlong internship at the HTC. Jessica worked as a case manager for three and a half years before she was hired as the director of Depaul USA New Orleans in 2018. Jessica enjoys spending time with family, friends and, especially, her 15-year-old son. She loves the New Orleans Saints and also going on road trips to Pearl Jam concerts and the beach. At the age of 17, she was in a car accident that left her paralyzed and wheelchair bound. That accident taught many valuable lessons, most notably, resilience, overcoming adversity and, interestingly, how a weakness can also be a strength. Jessica now understands her disability as a strength that motivates and empowers many people whose paths she crosses.

**Sterling and Maggie Millet** are lifelong New Orleanians. Both have service-oriented degrees - Sterling's in sociology and religious education, and Maggie's in elementary and high school education. Married 50 years, they have three sons and five grandchildren and are members of St. Joseph Parish. Volunteering has been part of their journey, including sacramental preparation at church, coaching, officiating youth sports, and helping with Sister Vera Butler's Feed Jesus program, which served as the introduction to the Rebuild Center and to their services for those in need.

Jessica Lovell            Sterling and Maggie Millet

**Beth Monahan** is the kitchen coordinator at Lantern Light Ministry. Before moving to New Orleans in 2014, she lived in New York and worked as a research scientist with Corning, Inc. She and her husband had vacationed here over the years and planned for New Orleans to be their snowbird home. Her husband died before this could become a reality. Beth moved to New Orleans afterwards and quickly started looking for volunteer opportunities. She soon accepted fellow volunteer David Hardin's invitation to volunteer at Lantern Light. Beth was hired as an employee in 2015 under Sister Vera Butler's direction and has been there ever since.

**Claire Mulligan** came to the Rebuild Center in 2020 as a Jesuit Volunteer placed with Depaul USA New Orleans. From Pennsylvania with a degree in biochemistry from Fairfield University, a Jesuit institution in Connecticut, she is now employed as Depaul's housing/wellness coordinator.

**Michael O'Connell** coordinated the shower services for the HTC in his role as the Jesuit Volunteer in 2018-19. A Bostonian and avid Patriots and Bruins fan, Mike graduated from Boston College in 2016 with majors in accounting and philosophy followed by two years as a public accountant. After moving to New Orleans, Mike fell in love with the city and the culture of New Orleans. Mike is now back in Boston, pursuing a master's in social work degree at Boston College, working in homeless services, while still cheering for the Saints.

Beth Monahan       Claire Mulligan       Michael O'Connell

**Sr. Anna Raimon** is a sister of the Presentation of the Blessed Virgin Mary Congregation of New Windsor, N.Y. Over the years, she taught in area schools in Massachusetts and in Cape Coast, Ghana in West Africa. In 2009, she joined the staff of Lantern Light Ministry. She currently resides at Presentation Convent in Leominster, Massachusetts.

**Eva Sohl** is the assistant director of the HTC. She first became involved with the center in 2016 through the "Tiny House Project" which ultimately housed eight unhoused persons over a period of two years. This experience inspired her to pursue her master's degree in social work from Southern University in New Orleans. As a part of her studies, Eva interned at the HTC and then with Depaul USA New Orleans. Eva earned a bachelor's degree in political science, history, and ethnic studies from the University of Nebraska.

**B.B. St. Roman** helped to establish the New Orleans Police Department Homeless Assistance Unit in 2004. Prior to that, she traveled the world, working on documentaries involving shamans, Buddhist monks and Mother Teresa. She was Dr. John's road manager for many years. B.B. continues to volunteer with the Homeless Assistance Unit and is an honorary staff member of the Rebuild Center.

Sr. Anna Raimon          Eva Sohl          B.B. St. Roman

**Fr. Thomas Stehlik** joined the Vincentian order of priests in 1989. What attracted him to Vincentian life was that the men were down-to-earth, humble, well-educated individuals with a missionary spirit who worked closely with the laity. Fr. Tom's Vincentian ministry has been largely influenced by working for 20 years with the Hispanic immigrant community, principally in Arkansas. He has served as the pastor of St. Joseph's Parish in New Orleans since 2011, serving on the leadership team of the Rebuild Center and fostering an active Lay Vincentian Program.

**Sr. Enid Storey** was a Sister of the Presentation of the Blessed Virgin Mary congregation. For many years, she ministered to the poor with Lantern Light Ministry, the Feed Jesus Program and the Rebuild Center. Previously, she served as a nurse in parish ministry at St. Clare's in the Bronx, as a teacher in New Jersey/New York and at the Dwelling Place of New York City, a shelter for homeless women. Sister Enid was an excellent storyteller whose stories were filled with humor and grace. She died unexpectedly in 2020 after returning to New York from New Orleans.

Fr. Thomas Stehlik          Sr. Enid Storey

**Bruce Vara** was born and raised in Norfolk, Va. In 1977, he moved to South Carolina on a full soccer college scholarship, where he also worked full-time. After college, Bruce lived in New York and eventually made his way down south to New Orleans. He met and married a young woman and moved to Atlanta to support her work. She later broke his heart. When asked why he returned to New Orleans after the break-up, Bruce said, "Part of my heart was here, and also for work." Life circumstances, not always kind, would introduce Bruce to homelessness in 2008. He was homeless for eight years until entering one of Depaul's housing programs. These days, Bruce spends much of his time reading and writing.

Originally from St. Louis, **Emily Bussen Wain** graduated from Rockhurst University in Kansas City. She served as a Jesuit Volunteer at the Harry Tompson Center from 2004-2005. When plans were made to reopen the center after Hurricane Katrina, Emily moved back to New Orleans to serve as the assistant director. She held this position from 2007 until 2020 when she was hired as the agency's executive director. Emily is a Licensed Master Social Worker and has a master's degree from LSU's School of Social Work. Emily met her husband, Travis Wain, while he was volunteering at the center and they now have a son together, Jackson Wain.

Bruce Vara                    Emily Bussen Wain

**Kahlise Ward** joined the Harry Tompson Center team in 2017 as the site coordinator for the Community Resource and Referral Center. During her three years with the center, Kahlise managed a full-time student schedule, earning her master's degree in social work from Southern University of New Orleans in 2020. She is now employed by Covenant House New Orleans as a human trafficking survivor advocate and enjoys helping disadvantaged youth and young adults experiencing homelessness.

**Kevin Wilson** has been a center assistant for Harry Tompson Center's satellite unit at the Community Resource and Referral Center for over three years. Originally from Jackson, Miss., he has lived in New Orleans since 2015. Kevin is known for his big smile, great laugh, and constant determination to brighten the day of everyone he meets.

**Juston Winfield** is an artist in New Orleans. Calling his art style "Neo-Impressionist," Juston has an eclectic art style, which mixes several subject matters in one piece. He uses found objects for his canvasses and paint frames. His new slogan is "Simplicity is complexity and imperfection is perfection on my surface." Juston's artworks have been exhibited at the New Orleans Museum of Art and at the Rebuild Center.

Kahlise Ward          Kevin Wilson          Juston Winfield

# About Vicki Judice

Born and raised in Baton Rouge, Vicki Judice graduated from LSU with a master's in social work, followed by a year as a Catholic lay volunteer in Los Angeles with Trinity Missions.

In 1982, she moved to New Orleans where she worked with the Parish Social Ministry Program of Catholic Charities and then with UNITY of Greater New Orleans helping to coordinate housing and services and to advocate for the reduction and prevention of homelessness. She was the executive director of the Harry Tompson Center 2013-2020.

Vicki is married to John Koeferl. Together, they raised three children in the Holy Cross and Gentilly Terrace neighborhoods.